LIVING
WILLS
AND WILLS

LIVING WILLS AND WILLS

HOWARD E. GOLDFLUSS

WINGS BOOKS
New York • Avenel, New Jersey

This 1994 edition is published by Wings Books, distributed by Random House Value Publishing, Inc., 40 Engelhard Avenue, Avenel, New Jersey 07001, by arrangement with the author.

Random House
New York • Toronto • London • Sydney • Auckland

Printed and bound in the United States of America

Library of Congress Cataloging-in-Publication Data
Goldfluss, Howard E.
  Wills and living wills / Howard E. Goldfluss.
    p. cm.
  ISBN 0-517-10145-9
  1. Right to die—United States—Popular works. I. Title.
KF3827.E87G65   1994
344.73′04197—dc20
[347.3044197]   94-8561
                                                                  CIP

8 7 6 5 4 3 2 1

Contents

LIVING WILLS

Introduction

Living Wills

"I like to think that I have lived meaningfully. I do not fear death. What I do fear is the possibility that my death will not be as meaningful as my life."

This quote from a listener of WOR's radio show "Tell it to the Judge" says it all. It represents the sentiment of the majority of the public.

In Part I of this book—**Living Wills**—I talk at length about the patient's right to choose "death with dignity" as has been mandated in courts throughout the country. The living will is a powerful instrument that can ensure that a patient's personal feelings about medical treatment and the prolongation of life will be honored. (In Part II of the book, I discuss wills and trusts. Any adult with dependents and/or assets would be wise to prepare a Last Will and Testament or a Living Trust.)

My immediate audience, in this first part of the book, are those individuals who are catastrophically ill and may be facing physical and/or mental incapacitation and imminent death. However, I strongly suggest that all adults, either currently healthy or living with a serious illness, make a living will.

In a recent *People* magazine interview with Bill and Hillary Clinton, Mrs. Clinton explained how her experiences had led her to conclude much the same thing: "Most of us still will not talk about death, will not talk about the process of dying. And so we don't share our feelings with our friends and family, particularly family members, who are often put into the position of having to make very difficult, painful decisions without knowing what their loved ones would want. And so part of what I came away from those experiences with was a feeling that we had to do that," she said, "that" being to make out a living will.

The living will may become a necessity for all of us. One of the key cases that I cite in this book—one that helped create the laws regarding patients' rights—is the *Cruzan* case. The patient was young and healthy. Then a car accident left her in a permanent vegetative state and her parents in a battle with the medical and legal establishment to discontinue life support. This was clearly a case where a living will was necessary. It would have given Ms. Cruzan the "right to die," spared her parents unnecessary pain, and kept the medical and legal bureaucracies out of what should have been a private right of passage. In the end, a living will would have given Ms. Cruzan control over her death, much as she had had control in her life.

Many of the other cases I cite, and much of my discussions in the first part of the book, center on individuals who are already in vegetative states—with irreversible physical and mental incapacitation—or in the end-stages of a terminal illness. These are immediate and often extreme examples of why a living will is so important. However, I have specifically cited the *Cruzan* case here to underscore the need for healthy individuals to consider executing a living will in the eventuality of a sudden illness or accident.

Indeed, the issue of all patients' rights—regardless of a person's health—is an especially critical one in the current healthcare climate that demands cost containment on the one hand, but fears malpractice on the other. Part I of this book will answer many general questions about your patient rights, both in and outside the hospital.

The courts and the state legislatures have established that you have the right to make a choice. The Supreme Court labels it a Constitutional right. And well it should! This humane concept gives you the absolute right to refuse life-sustaining treatment if you become terminally ill, brain dead, suffer an irreversible condition accompanied by unceasing pain, or are otherwise unable to function normally.

You can express your intent in a living will and/or health care proxy—written instruments that give someone else the right to make decisions for you if you are incapable of doing so.

The law does not require you to be kept alive in a vegetative state through artificial means. Nor does it require your loved ones to watch you die without dignity.

Obviously, a decision of this nature cannot be made lightly. The seriousness of this step is self-evident. It is important that you discuss it with your doctor and your family. There may be some who have philosophical, ethical, or other considerations that will enter into their thinking before they can contemplate a living will. Also, please remember that the courts have held that *clear and convincing* evidence must be established, preferably in the form of a written instrument, of intent to discontinue treatment. If you have a clear intent that you refuse to exist without truly living, then follow the procedures set forth here.

The many letters that I have received concerning this subject indicate a precise awareness that none of us is immortal and that our lives will end at some point. The choice of how we die was not made available to us until fairly recently. Hopefully, the exercise of this choice will eliminate the frightening anticipation of dying without dignity.

CHAPTER 1

Living Wills and Health Care Proxies

"THE TIMING OF DEATH, ONCE A MATTER OF FATE, IS NOW A MATTER OF CHOICE."

So wrote Justice William Brennan in the 1990 landmark Supreme Court case of *Cruzan v. Missouri*. With these words, the court gave legal and moral recognition to the basic right of an individual to determine how he or she will die.

Understandably, death is not a subject that most people like to discuss. Yet, more Americans are facing the prospect and are determined to choose the manner and the conditions under which they will die. Exercising the option of choosing how one dies isn't—and shouldn't be—reserved only for the catastrophically ill. Healthy individuals must also consider their choices regarding medical treatment in the face of a sudden and serious illness or accident. It is not surprising, therefore, that currently there is great interest in dying with dignity, and in minimizing the physical pain of the final stages of terminal illness and the emotional pain of family and friends.

There are legal precautions that you may take to avoid a prolonged death. Documents such as the living will and the health care proxy are most often used to achieve this purpose.

Living Will

The living will is a directive to your medical providers—doctor, technician, nurse, hospital—and your family. It must be made and executed when you are in sound mind and capable of executing the instrument. Healthy individuals, who know their legal rights regarding living wills, and are not emotionally constrained by the prospect of physical and mental incapacity, have a clear advantage in being able to execute specific and informed medical directives. Further, such directives are not valid if you are physically and mentally able to participate in decisions regarding your medical care. They apply only when you are in an irreversible mental or physical terminal condition with no reasonable expectation of recovery, or when you are permanently unconscious, or have suffered irreversible brain damage, with the certainty that you will never regain the ability to make decisions or express your wishes about medical treatment.

It is important to note here that the above medical conditions will be, almost without exception, the *only* conditions under which another individual will make medical decisions for you, including the termination of life support. And these extreme conditions are not the norm. We often, and mistakenly, equate the terms "terminal" and "incurable" with incapacity and imminent death. The tens of thousands of individuals who live with medical diagnoses of incurable and/or terminal illnesses might disagree. Many people with cancer, AIDS, Alzheimer's, Huntington's chorea, and multiple sclerosis, among others, can and do enjoy productive, quality lives, sometimes for years after their original diagnoses.

However, in the eventuality that you do become physically and/or mentally incapacitated, you have the right to direct your medical treatment so that it is limited to measures that keep you comfortable and relieve pain.

While the law does not require that you be specific in the written instrument about which particular treatments you would refuse, it is important to know what form these treatments can take.

Cardiopulmonary Resuscitation (CPR)

CPR is a treatment that restarts the heart after it stops beating. The condition is commonly referred to as cardiac or pulmonary arrest.

The treatment involves manual pressure and the application of electric shocks to the chest, known as defibrillation. It also involves the injection of intravenous drugs to restart the heart and return the blood pressure to normal.

In hopeless cases, cardiopulmonary arrest allows death to occur peacefully. You may, therefore, wish to provide in your living will or health proxy that you do *not* want CPR to be administered if you are in the final stages of a terminal and irreversible medical condition.

Mechanical Respiration

A machine called a respirator or ventilator can take over breathing if the lungs do not function adequately, supplying oxygen through a tube inserted in the windpipe.

There are times when ventilation can help pull a person through a serious illness such as pneumonia and restore the previous level of functioning. But in some cases, normal breathing can never be restored, and the patient becomes dependent upon mechanical ventilation.

The latter is a condition to which you may "just say no." You may feel that being permanently hooked up to a machine with no hope of leaving your bed is not truly living. You may therefore specify in your living will or health care proxy that you do not wish ventilation to be administered.

If you choose to forego that treatment, you can add a directive that states though you do *not* wish mechanical respiration to be administered if it only prolongs the dying process, you do want all other measures to be administered to keep you comfortable, including oxygen, sedation, or medication as needed.

Tube Feeding

Tube feeding is a process used for patients who are unable (or unwilling) to swallow food and fluids. It feeds artificial nutrients through a tube inserted into the digestive system. It is often given to persons who are unconscious or severely brain damaged and unable to tell the physician whether they are hungry or thirsty.

This is another classic example of existing without truly living. It is an artificial prolongation of the dying process that also prolongs the misery for you and your loved ones. You may wish to specify in your directive that if you become so stricken, you do not want tube feeding or other means of maintaining life unless it is to make you more comfortable.

Antibiotics

Serious infection in dying or brain-damaged people can lead to a coma even before other symptoms of infection occur. This may be the body's method of producing a peaceful death. By curing the infection, the antibiotic may make the hopelessly ill person more fully aware of his or her discomfort. You therefore may wish to specify in your living will or health proxy that you do *not* want antibiotic administration if it merely prolongs the dying process.

Surgical Procedure

If you are in an advanced or final stage of a terminal illness, you may be faced with the choice of surgery as a means of pain reduction. However, your doctor may conclude that the same result could be obtained through pain medication. Under these circumstances, you may direct that no surgery be performed.

Chemotherapy and Radiation

Chemotherapy is drug treatment for cancer. It often causes nausea, vomiting, or other serious complications. Sometimes, it temporarily reduces the discomfort of a cancer, even if it does not cure it.

Radiation therapy uses high doses of radiation to shrink or eliminate tumors. Although it produces side effects, it is generally better tolerated than chemotherapy.

With some forms of cancer, recurrence after a series of anticancer treatments may mean that the cancer is incurable and further treatment may at most prolong life for a relatively short time. You may wish to provide that under such circumstances you do not want further chemotherapy or radiation unless it serves to reduce pain. However, you should also include a provision that if new drugs and/or surgical techniques become available to treat your disease, you may exercise your option to resume treatment.

Comfort Care

You may wish to specify that any kind of treatment that increases your physical or emotional comfort is requested. Such a request gives the medical personnel wide discretion in administering sufficient doses of medication to ease your pain.

These are some of the directives that you can make about your future medical treatment. It would be wise to discuss specifics with your physician. There may be more suggestions he or she could make about what should be included.

Naturally, the status of your condition—whether you are in a life-threatening or irreversible condition—is a medical judgment. In a living will, you set forth directives that the doctor and hospital must follow, as is true with a health care proxy. In most instances the diagnosis of your condition is clear enough for your directives to be followed. But there may be circumstances where the prognosis is not that clear cut, and an option has to be exercised. It is understandable that your physician may not want to assume that responsibility. That is why I recommend that in addition to the living will you designate a health care proxy, who will assume that responsibility after conferring with the physician.

Health Care Proxy

This instrument, sometimes referred to as a Durable Power of Attorney, differs from the living will in that a health care agent is designated to carry out your wishes and to make decisions that you are unable to because of your incapacitation. As discussed in the section on living wills, healthy individuals should also select a health care proxy, in the event of illness or accident.

The forms included in the following chapter indicate the difference between the two instruments. The vast majority of states accept and recognize living wills and health care proxies. Some recognize one and not the other. Consult the map in the next chapter, which sets forth the present state of the law in each of the fifty states.

Generally, you may give the person you select as your *health care agent* as much or as little authority as you wish. You may give him or her the widest discretion or limit that discretion to specified treatments. You can fashion your directives in any way you choose. This is an individual decision—made alone—after serious contemplation about the entire concept. The point is that it is totally *your choice*, and that you will have more control over your death.

When you choose your agent, be sure it is someone whose judgment you trust and who is willing to accept the responsibility that goes with the designation. It may be a family member—or it may not.

You are the best judge of whom to choose to exercise

the option to stop treatment and to preserve your wish to die with dignity.

After reading the living will and health care forms, you will see that the procedure is not complicated. A lawyer is generally not required, only two adult witnesses to your signature. Nevertheless, you may wish to consult an attorney for any suggestions that he or she may make. You may use the form I have included, but you don't have to. You can express your intent in any manner that you wish as long as it is clearly spelled out. No formal language is required.

You may give your health care agent unlimited authority or you may limit it in anyway you choose.

It is a wise practice to appoint an alternate health care agent in the event that your designated agent is not available when a decision must be made. However, doctors, hospitals, technicians, and all medical personnel are required to follow any instructions in your health care proxy form, even in the absence of your proxy, as long as they are made aware of the existence of the proxy and the instructions contained therein are clear.

It is important to remember that your proxy may not make any decisions concerning your treatment until your doctor tells him or her that you are unable to make such decisions. Also keep in mind that your instructions in a living will or health care proxy are not carved in stone. You can change your mind. You can revoke the proxy. You can change treatment instructions. You can substitute another person as proxy. Just fill out a new form. The previous one is automatically revoked.

You may limit the authority of your health care agent to provide that the proxy will expire on a certain date.

Otherwise, if not revoked, the proxy will be valid indefinitely.

If you have chosen your spouse as your health care agent and you become divorced or legally separated, your proxy is automatically canceled. It would be prudent to appoint another agent immediately.

Your agent need not be concerned about personal liability for treatment decisions made in good faith on your behalf. Your agent also cannot be held liable for the cost of your care just because he or she is your agent.

After the living will and/or health care proxy is executed, before at least two witnesses, make several copies. Of course, you will want one, and so will your agent. In addition, it would be wise to send a copy to your physician, and your attorney, and have one ready to present to the hospital at the time of admission.

There is a solid reason to be as specific as possible in these instruments. I opened this chapter with a quote from Justice William Brennan in the *Cruzan* case. While the Supreme Court did accept the person's right to choose, it also stated that Missouri, or any other state, has the right to require "clear and convincing" evidence that the comatose patient would have decided to forego life support. While Nancy Cruzan had a constitutionally protected right to refuse unwanted medical treatment, there was no "clear and convincing" evidence that such was her intention. All that was submitted was supposition by her parents and the guardian appointed by the court. It was probably a correct supposition, but it did not pass the "clear and convincing" test.

The court, in effect, sent a mixed signal. Yes, you can choose to end your pain. You can demand that life-sustaining treatment be withheld, but there must be something clear and convincing that could establish in a courtroom that such was your intent. The existence of a living will or health care proxy would have changed the *Cruzan* decision. It is the kind of evidence that is crucial in asserting your right to choose how you die.

CHAPTER 2

The Moral Issue

Whether you are currently healthy, living with an incurable illness, or facing the prospect of incapacitation, hopefully the first two chapters of this book have helped you to come to grips with the reality that you are not immortal. You have taken the necessary steps, through a living will or health care proxy, to insure that when the time comes, you will die with dignity. You probably will be comfortable with that knowledge. But what about the one you have designated to make the decision on granting consent to the cessation of life-sustaining procedures. Will he or she be troubled by a conscience that questions the morality of this consent? Does it challenge his or her religious beliefs? Is it just plain wrong?

Any individual who has to deal with the burden of terminating a life would have to have these self-doubts. Nevertheless, reading the statements and positions taken by medical, legal, and religious authorities *can* help clear his or her conscience.

On March 15, 1986, the Council on Ethical and Judicial Affairs of the American Medical Association (AMA) issued a major opinion that allowed physicians and medical personnel, equally troubled, to breathe easier. The report declared that it is ethically permissible for doctors to withold all life-support treatment, including artificial nutrition and hydration, from permanently unconscious or dying patients.

Although there had been prior declarations of this nature by private physicians, this was the first time that the largest medical organization in the nation had given its official sanction. Following the AMA's course, the American Academy of Neurology stated shortly thereafter:

> Persistent vegetative state patients do not have the capacity to experience pain or suffering. . . . Medical treatment, including the medical provisions of artificial nutrition and hydration, provides no benefit to patients once the diagnosis has been established to a high degree of certainty.

Similar reports have been issued by the American Dietetic Association, the American Society of Parenteral and Enteral Nutrition (ASPN), as well as a number of state medical societies (California, Massachusetts, Minnesota, New York, Oregon, Texas, Washington, and Wisconsin).

Doubts about the propriety in relieving pain and suffering of the terminally ill patient by withholding or withdrawing artificial fluids have been put to rest. "Painless and peaceful" is how two physician coauthors described death from water deficiency, and they added:

"Tube feeding for an extended period of time appears far more distressing." (Christine K. Cassel, MD and David T. Walls, MD, *Journal of the American Geriatric Society*, March 1984.)

An article in *Nursing Magazine* of January 1983 goes further—taking the position that reduction of fluids can bring relief of symptoms of vomiting, coughing, and edema and can "serve almost as a natural anesthetic." ("The Dehydration Question," Joyce V. Zerewkh, RN, MA.)

When Paul Brophy was permitted to die eight days after feeding had been stopped, his wife described his death as "peaceful—he just stopped breathing." His doctor said, "You'd walk into that hospital room and there was a quiet dignity—a peacefulness there. It was by no means a violent death." ("Brophy Revisited—His Physician's View of Pain and Suffering," Lawrence J. Lebowitz, *Massachusetts Medicine,* Jan–Feb 1987.)

These reported comments were connected with the well-publicized Massachusetts case where a court approved the cessation of Paul Brophy's tube feeding, finding that "people in his condition (persistent vegetative state) do not feel pain, and that an unwarranted tube can be intrusive and extraordinary."

Clearly, the courts have adopted the position of the medical community in relation to cessation of tubular feeding. Listen to the United States Supreme Court in the *Cruzan* case:

> Whether or not the techniques used to pass food and water into the patient's alimentary tract are termed "medical treatment," it is clear that they all involve

some degree of intrusion and restraint. Requiring a competent adult to endure such procedures against her will burdens the patient's liberty, dignity, and freedom to determine the course of her own treatment.

A New York court, in *Delio v. Westchester County Medical Center* in 1987, could not have expressed it more emphatically: "Clearly, there is no benefit to the State in prolonging Daniel's existence under circumstances he would have found demeaning."

There should be no doubt that the medical establishment's position is to support the moral right to cease artificial sustenance. The language is convincing:

I personally grieve to see non-responsive vegetative states perpetuated almost indefinitely by parenteral feeding. Unfortunately, the feeding tube is often initiated in the acute care setting without any realistic discussion of prognosis with the family or the responsible party. I have never spoken with an elderly patient who requested that such a vegetative state be maintained by artificial alimentation. ("Artificial Feeding—Laying to Rest Some Misconceptions," Stephen S. Cox, MD, *Hastings Center Report.*)

In the prestigious *Archives of Internal Medicine* (May 1983), Dr. Kenneth C. Micetich writes:

If death can be seen as a comfort as it would for the patients in our cases and their families, then ordering or continuing to use IV fluids may actually be seen as cruel. In fact, IV fluids may prolong the dying process just as effectively as using the respirator. If the latter is not morally required, then why should the former be so? ("Are Intravenous Fluids Morally Required for a Dying Patient?")

Dr. Sidney H. Wanzer, in the April 12, 1984 edition of the *New England Journal of Medicine* addresses the morality question regarding patients in a vegetative state.

It is morally justifiable to withhold antibiotics and artificial nutrition and hydration, as well as other forms of life sustaining treatment. . . . If food and water are rejected by mouth it is ethically permissible to withhold artificial nutrition by vein or gastric tube.

The argument that feeding must be given to brain-dead or terminally ill patients because it represents basic human care has no responsible support. Dr. Robert Steinbrook and Dr. Bernard Lo discuss alternatives in the February 4, 1988 issue of the *New England Journal of Medicine:*

Instead of using artificial feeding to show caring, plans can be made for supportive care, pain control, skin care, and personal hygiene. . . . The symptoms of hunger and thirst can be relieved by moistening the patient's lips with ice chips, or, when possible, with oral food and fluids.

It is a long-standing myth that religious groups, especially the Roman Catholic church, oppose the withholding of life-sustaining treatment for those clearly in a terminal state. This misconception tends to confuse those who adhere to the pro-life stance that is the firm tenet of the church. The cessation of life-sustaining medical procedures for the terminally ill cannot in any way be equated with the pro-life concept, and ecclessiastical experts clarify the distinction. As a matter of fact, the church, through its spokesmen, uses language similar to that of the medical profession. In the October 1986 edition of *Health Progress,* the Reverend James McCartney, PhD, states the church's position:

> A medical treatment that does not offer the hope of somehow restoring life or health is useless, and thus surely presents a burden without a countermanding benefit. . . . Thus Catholic teaching is not opposed to the withholding or withdrawal of artificial sustenance, when, in the patient's view, this intervention becomes physically, psychologically, economically, emotionally, or spiritually too difficult to bear either for the patient or others.

Thus, the church recognizes the humanity of allowing a peaceful death, and the inhumanity of maintaining a sorrowful and hopeless existence. But if you are a practicing Roman Catholic and are still disturbed by the possibility that this position could be contrary to the strong pro-life stance, then be comforted by the words of the Archbishop Joseph Cardinal Bernardin. His remarks were made before a gathering of physicians and Catholic laypeople in May 1988 at the Chicago Hospital. Keep in mind that his Eminence spoke these words as Chairman of the National Conference of Bishops' Committee for Pro-Life Activities:

We . . . may not develop a policy to keep alive those who should be allowed a natural death, that is, those who are terminally ill, or to preclude a decision—that the artificial provision of nutrition and hydration has become useless or unduly burdensome. I am convinced that from a moral point of view, the essential bond between food, water, and life argues convincingly for the presumption that nutrition and hydration should always be provided.

But I am also convinced that *we are not morally obliged* to do everything that is technically possible. There are cases where we should not be obliged artificially to provide nutrition and hydration. (emphasis added.)

Thus, one of the church's leading spokesman on its pro-life position puts to rest the incorrect belief that withholding sustenance in a hopeless case is a mortal sin. Those of the Catholic faith, and indeed of any faith who believe strongly in the sanctity of human life, need not torture themselves about the morality of allowing a loved one to die in peace.

CHAPTER 3

Honoring the Patient's Wishes

The first two chapters of this book speak directly to the patient facing an incapacitating illness, to his or her right to legally define medical directives that will ensure a more comfortable and dignified death, and to the need for the patient to designate a health care agent who will abide by those directives. It should be clear by now that serious thought must go into choosing the health care agent. A spouse or other family member may not be the optimal choice. Despite their best intentions, emotional attachment and false hope may prevent them from acting decisively when the moment to "choose death" arrives. A better choice for a health care agent might be a good friend with some medical knowledge, or even a health care professional not directly involved in the patient's medical treatment—a social worker, or a therapist, to name two examples.

Whatever his or her relationship is to the patient, the health care agent has agreed to assume a serious and unique responsibility. This chapter speaks directly to that individual and the role he or she will play in the patient's life and death.

Make no mistake about it. The carrying out of your duties as a health care agent will not be a piece of cake. You have taken on the responsibility of making the most vital of decisions. And you may encounter resistance. You may find, for example, that there will be a natural reluctance by the medical profession to accept, even in writing, the intention of the patient. In some instances, the reluctance is understandable. Doctors, nurses, hospitals—all medical personnel—worry about malpractice lawsuits that often result in seven-figure verdicts.

If there is any doubt about the language contained in the living will or health care proxy—if the directions are not absolutely clear, if something vital is omitted, or if any ambiguity exists—there could be resulting delay and noncompliance. It is therefore imperative that the instructions be as precise as possible.

It is equally important for you to fully understand the patient's condition. There are necessary questions that you must ask. Is the patient terminal? Is he or she conscious of what is happening? Is he or she in unceasing pain? Has the patient reached that point beyond recovery? Has the patient's condition stabilized, so the physician can respond to these queries?

If you are told that it is too soon to know for sure, ask when you can have a clear answer. As surrogate, you must be persistent. You have a legal right to this information.

Also, keep in mind that although there may be resistance, a living will or health care proxy must be honored if there is no ambiguity. The real problem that can cause litigation arises from the instances where no written instrument expressing the patient's wishes was executed. Naturally, there is a burden of proof that requires the validity of the oral expression of this intent.

In such a case, you must inform the physician about anything he or she said concerning the termination of life-sustaining treatment. If there were only oral statements of intent, questions will arise. If such statements were made, were the words spoken seriously? Were you given the impression that the patient was expressing a personal wish and not a general declaration of policy? And had the patient expressed his or her intentions about the course to take? Were there more conversations along those lines? Did other people hear those conversations?

Always remember the ruling of the United States Supreme Court in the *Cruzan* case. The Court held that the patient had an unequivocable right to terminate her life support if her wishes were expressed in advance in the form of "clear and convincing" evidence. Naturally, the signed document, living will or health care proxy (sometimes referred to as the durable power of attorney), is the strongest evidence of "clear and convincing" intent. But the law does not require expression of intent to be exclusively in written form. A dispute leading to a court determination could be decided by persuasive evidence such as more than one oral statement, detailed statements, or the degree of certainty. All could help persuade a judge who would eventually have the duty to render a decision.

There are several states that recognize the right of family or close associates of the patient to make medical decisions, even though no advance directions were given, written or oral. Under such circumstances, where the patient is in a permanently deteriorative state, you may be permitted to substitute your judgment, guided by the patient's beliefs and general values.

This would be a "substitution of judgment" case, and although it could stand up in court, the burden in such instance would be the greatest, if contested, to show that your judgment would indeed be similar to the patient's.

Questions arise as to the appropriate time to make decisions about the patient's life support. Obviously, the patient's condition must be stabilized so that a positive diagnosis (current medical condition) and prognosis (what is expected to occur) can be made. A lot would depend on the wording of the instrument that the patient executed. Some living wills provide that they are to take effect when the patient's condition is irreversible. Some provide that they apply only when the patient is "terminal" or "permanently unconscious."

To a layman, this could very well be a distinction without a difference. Yet to an expert, this could mean two different things. It is therefore wise to use all inclusive terminology in the written instruments, if that is the patient's intent.

It is essential that every medical person coming into contact with the patient be made aware of the existence of the living will or health care proxy—the attending physician, the nurses, the social workers, the patient representative, and hospital administrators. The more the better.

Is this an awesome responsibility? Absolutely. It demands that you place yourself in a heartbreaking situation, and you will be sacrificing your peace of mind. But remember the dedication to your goal—to bring peace to the patient, and not necessarily yourself. In many instances you will need reassurance and counseling. It is perfectly understandable if you cannot bear the burden of making this decision without being fully informed and that you may require moral support.

Most hospitals and nursing homes have patient representatives and/or social workers. They are there to assist you and will probably know the applicable law in your state.

It is important to keep in mind that this area of law is going through many changes and that laws on the various issues raised in connection with the living-will concept vary from state to state. Besides your state bar associations and medical societies, the following list of facilities are sources of reliable information. National groups are listed first, state and regional organizations follow, and finally there are maps indicating the status of each state on the various options.

Services are listed by the following codes:

C Case counseling
D Distribution of advance directives that conform to state law
E Educational programs and/or workshops
I Information and publications
R Referrals to legal or institutional resources
S Support groups and services

National Health Care Resources

HOSPICELINK
Hospice Education Institute
P.O. Box 713
Essex, CT 06426
1-800-331-1620
*Services: C, E, I, R (hospice programs) and
sympathetic listening.*

NATIONAL HOSPICE ORGANIZATION
1901 North Moore Street, Suite 901
Arlington, VA 22209
1-800-658-8898
Services: C, E, I, R (hospice programs)

VISITING NURSE ASSOCIATION OF AMERICA
3801 East Florida Avenue, Suite 206
Denver, CO 80210
1-800-426-2547
Services: R (hospice programs)

National Legal Issues

AARP LEGAL COUNSEL FOR THE ELDERLY
1909 K Street NW
Washington, DC 20049
202-833-6720
Services: C, E, I

AMERICAN BAR ASSOCIATION
1800 M Street NW, South Lobby
Washington, DC 20036
202-331-2200
Services: E, I

National Support Services

ALZHEIMER'S ASSOCIATION
919 North Michigan Avenue, Suite 1000
Chicago, IL 60611-1676
1-800-272-3900
312-335-8700
Services: I, S

ASSOCIATION FOR DEATH EDUCATION & COUNSELLING
638 Prospect Avenue
Hartford, CT 06105
203-232-4825
Services: I, R

CHILDREN OF AGING PARENTS
2761 Trenton Road
Levittown, PA 19056
215-945-6900
Services: I, R (social worker available), S

National Advocacy Information

CHOICE IN DYING, INC.
(The National Council for the Right to Die)
200 Varick Street
New York, NY 10014
212-366-5540
Services: C, D, E, I, R (all inclusive)

National Ethics

THE HASTING CENTER
255 Elm Road
Briarcliff Manor, NY 10510
914-762-8500
Services: E, I, R

Northeast Region

CONNECTICUT STATE DEPARTMENT ON AGING
175 Main Street
Hartford, CT 06106
203-566-3238
Services: D, R

MAINE HEALTH CARE DECISIONS PROJECT
The Acadia Institute
118 West Street
Bar Harbor, ME 04609
207-288-4082

MASSACHUSETTS HEALTH DECISIONS
P.O. Box 417
Sharon, MA 02067
617-784-1966
Services: D, E, I

VERMONT ETHICS NETWORK
103 South Main Street
Waterbury, VT
Services: D, E, I, R, S

Middle Atlantic Region

LEGAL HOTLINE FOR ELDERLY D.C. RESIDENTS
(AARP/LEGAL COUNSEL FOR THE ELDERLY)
601 E Street NW
Washington, DC 20049
202-234-0970
Services: C, D, E, I

MARYLAND OFFICE ON AGING
301 West Preston Street, 10th Floor
Baltimore, MD 21201
Services: D (please write for information)

NJ CITIZENS COMMITTEE ON BIOMEDICAL ETHICS
120 Morris Avenue
Summit, NJ 17901
Services: E, I

NEW YORK TASK FORCE ON LIFE AND THE LAW
P.O. Box 1634
New York, NY 10116-1634
Services: D, I (please write for information)

FRIENDS/RELATIVES OF THE INSTITUTIONALIZED AGED
11 John Street, Suite 601
New York, NY 10038
212-732-4455
Services: C, D, I

COALITION OF ADVOCATES FOR THE RIGHTS OF THE
INFIRM ELDERLY (CARIE)
1315 Walnut Street, Suite 1000
Philadelphia, PA 19107
215-545-5728
Services: C, E, I, R

Southeast Region

ARKANSAS MEDICAL ASSOCIATION
P.O. Box 5776
Little Rock, AR 72215
501-224-8967
Services: D

UNIVERSITY OF ARKANSAS FOR MEDICAL SERVICES
Division of Medical Humanities
4301 West Markham, MS 646
Little Rock, AR 72205
501-686-5622
Services: D, E, I

GEORGIA HEALTH DECISIONS
1720 Peachtree Street
Atlanta, GA 30309
404-874-9327
Services: C, D, E, I, R

LOUISIANA OFFICE OF ELDERLY AFFAIRS
4550 North Boulevard
Baton Rouge, LA 70898
504-935-1700
Services: I, R

MISSISSIPPI DEPARTMENT OF HUMAN
SERVICES
Division of Aging and Adult Services
421 West Pascagoula
Jackson, MS 39203
1-800-345-6347 (in Mississippi)
601-949-2070
Services: E, I

NORTH CAROLINA MEDICAL SOCIETY
P.O. Box 27167
Raleigh, NC 27611
704-332-4421
Services: D, I

BIOETHICS RESOURCE GROUP
118 Colonial Avenue
Charlotte, NC 28207
704-332-4421

CENTER FOR CLINICAL/RESEARCH ETHICS
Vanderbilt University School of Medicine
CCC-5319 Medical Center North
Nashville, TN 37232
615-322-2252
Services: C, D, E, I

Midwest Region

INDIANA DEPARTMENT OF HUMAN
SERVICES
Aging and In-Home Services
P.O. Box 7089
Indianapolis, IN 46207
317-232-7020
Services: I, R

KANSAS DEPARTMENT ON AGING
Docking State Office Building, 122
915 SW Harrison
Topeka, KS 66612-1500
1-800-432-3535 (in Kansas)
913-296-4986
Services: D, E, I, R

MICHIGAN MEDICAL SELF-DETERMINATION ASSOCIATION
P.O. Box 8148
Ann Arbor, MI 48107
313-971-4200
Services: D, E (including speakers), I

MINNESOTA ETHICS NETWORK
Minnesota Health Association
221 University Avenue SE, Suite 425
Minneapolis, MN 55414
612-331-5571
Services: C, D, E, I, R

MINNESOTA BOARD ON AGING
444 Lafayette Road
St. Paul, MN 55155-3843
1-800-652-9747 (in Minnesota)
612-296-2770
Services: D, E, I, R, S

MIDWEST BIOETHICS CENTER
410 Archibald, Suite 200
Kansas City, MO 64111
816-756-2713
Services: D, E, I

LINCOLN MEDICAL EDUCATION
FOUNDATION
4600 Valley Road
Lincoln, NE 68510
402-483-4581
Services: E, I, R

WISCONSIN HEALTH DECISIONS
P.O. Box 511
Madison, WI 53701-0511
Services: D, E, I (please write for information)

THE CENTER FOR THE STUDY OF BIOETHICS AND
WISCONSIN ETHICS COMMITTEE
8701 Watertown Plank Road
Milwaukee, WI 53226
414-257-8498
Services: C, E, I, R (including speakers and library)

Southwest Region

ARIZONA HEALTH DECISIONS
P.O. Box 4401
Prescott, AZ 86302
602-778-4850
Services: C, D, E, I, R, S

DOROTHY GARSKE CENTER
4250 East Camelback Road, Suite 185 K
Phoenix, AZ 85018

PIMA COUNCIL ON AGING
2919 East Broadway
Tucson, AZ 85716
602-952-1464
Services: C, D, I, R

NEW MEXICO OMBUDSMAN'S OFFICE
224 East Palace Avenue
La Villa Rivera Building
Santa Fe, NM 87501
505-827-7634
Services: I, R

NEW MEXICO HEALTH DECISIONS
2801 Lomas NE
Albuquerque, NM 87106
505-255-9559
Services: D, E

TEXAS MEDICAL ASSOCIATION
Department of Medical Ethics
401 W. 15th Street
Austin, TX 78701
512-370-1300
Services: D, I

BENEDECTINE HEALTH RESORT CENTER
530 Bandera Road
San Antonio, TX 78228
512-735-4988
Services: I (legal information)

Western Region

CALIFORNIA HEALTH DECISIONS
505 South Main Street, Suite 400
Orange, CA 92668
714-647-4920
Services: D, E, I

COLORADO CENTER FOR HEALTH ETHICS AND POLICY
University of Colorado, Denver
1445 Market Street, Suite 380Q
Denver, CO 80202
303-820-5640
Services: C, E, I, R

OREGON HEALTH DECISIONS
921 SW Washington, Suite 723
Portland, OR 97205
503-241-0744
Services: D, E, I, R

COUNSELING, EDUCATION, AND PASTORAL CARE
St. Lukes Medical Center
2285 116th Avenue NE
Bellevue, WA 98004
206-455-5515
Services: C

Hawaii

KOKUA COUNCIL FOR SENIOR CITIZENS
EDUCATION FUND
3135 Oahu Avenue
Honolulu, HA 96822
808-988-5813
Services: D, I

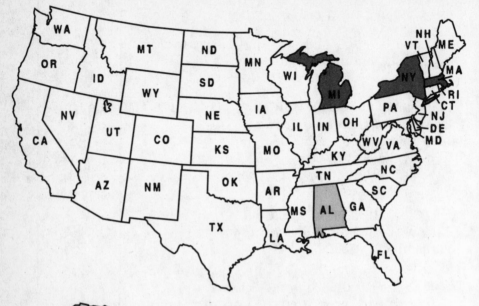

STATE STATUTES GOVERNING LIVING WILLS AND APPOINTMENT OF HEALTH CARE AGENTS

Jurisdictions with legislation that authorizes both living wills and the appointment of a health care agent (the District of Columbia and 45 states: Arizona, Arkansas, California, Colorado, Connecticut, Delaware, Florida, Georgia, Hawaii, Idaho, Illinois, Indiana, Iowa, Kansas, Kentucky, Louisiana, Maine, Maryland, Minnesota, Mississippi, Missouri, Montana, Nebraska, Nevada, New Hampshire, New Jersey, New Mexico, North Carolina, North Dakota, Ohio, Oklahoma, Oregon, Pennsylvania, Rhode Island, South Carolina, South Dakota, Tennessee, Texas, Utah, Vermont, Virginia, Washington, West Virginia, Wisconsin and Wyoming).

States with legislation that authorizes only living wills (2 states: Alabama and Alaska).

States with legislation that authorizes only the appointment of a health care agent (3 states: Massachusetts, Michigan and New York).

Note: The specifics of living will and health care agent legislation vary greatly from state to state. In addition, many states also have court-made law that affects residents' rights. For information about specific state laws, please contact Choice In Dying.

© **Choice In Dying, Inc.** (formerly Concern for Dying/Society for the Right to Die) 200 Varick Street, 10th Floor   New York, NY 10014-4810   212-366-5540

STATE STATUTES GOVERNING
SURROGATE DECISIONMAKING

☐ Jurisdictions with statutes authorizing surrogate decisionmaking in the absence of advance directives (the District of Columbia and 23 states: Arizona, Arkansas, Colorado, Connecticut, Florida, Illinois, Indiana, Iowa, Louisiana, Maine, Maryland, Montana, Nevada, New Mexico, North Carolina, Ohio, Oregon, South Carolina, Texas, Utah, Virginia, West Virginia and Wyoming).

■ States without statutes governing surrogate decisionmaking (27 states: Alabama, Alaska, California, Delaware, Georgia, Hawaii, Idaho, Kansas, Kentucky, Massachusetts, Michigan, Minnesota, Mississippi, Missouri, Nebraska, New Hampshire, New Jersey, New York, North Dakota, Oklahoma, Pennsylvania, Rhode Island, South Dakota, Tennessee, Vermont, Washington and Wisconsin).

© **Choice In Dying, Inc.** (formerly Concern for Dying/Society for the Right to Die) 200 Varick Street, 10th Floor   New York, NY 10014-4810   212-366-5540

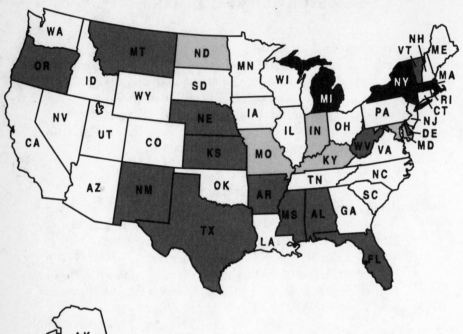

ARTIFICIAL NUTRITION AND HYDRATION
IN LIVING WILL STATUTES

☐ States with living will statutes that permit individuals to refuse artificial nutrition and hydration through their living wills (29 states: Alaska, Arizona[1], California, Colorado, Connecticut, Georgia, Hawaii, Idaho, Illinois[2], Iowa, Louisiana, Maine, Minnesota, Nevada, New Jersey, New Hampshire, North Carolina, Ohio, Oklahoma, Pennsylvania, Rhode Island, South Carolina, South Dakota, Tennessee, Utah, Virginia, Washington, Wisconsin and Wyoming).

☐ States with living will statutes that require the provision of nutrition and hydration except in very limited circumstances (5 states: Indiana[3], Kentucky, Maryland[4], Missouri[3] and North Dakota).

■ Jurisdictions whose living will statutes do not explicitly permit the refusal of, or explicitly require the application of artificial nutrition and hydration (the District of Columbia and 13 states: Alabama, Arkansas, Delaware, Florida, Kansas, Mississippi, Montana, Nebraska, New Mexico, Oregon, Texas, Vermont and West Virginia).

■ States without living will statutes (3 states: Massachusetts, Michigan and New York).

[1]The authority to withhold or withdraw artificial nutrition and hydration is only explicitly mentioned in the sample document.

[2]Artificial nutrition and hydration cannot be withheld or withdrawn if the resulting death is due to starvation or dehydration.

[3]The medical power of attorney statutes in Indiana and Missouri permit appointed agents to refuse artificial nutrition and hydration on behalf of the principal.

[4]Although the act requires the "administration of food and water," a Maryland Attorney General's Opinion has stated that artificial nutrition and hydration may be refused through a living will.

© **Choice In Dying, Inc.** (formerly Concern for Dying/Society for the Right to Die) 200 Varick Street, 10th Floor   New York, NY   10014-4810   212-366-5540

The maps on pages 40–45 indicate the various state statutes on:

1. Living wills and appointment
   of health care agents
2. Surrogate or family decisions
   without advance directives
3. Artificial nutrition and hydration in living wills

Although a state statute may be silent on a particular authorization, court decisions in the state may have specifically accepted what a statute had not. For example, although New York's statute only authorizes the appointment of health care agents, the courts have approved the living will as clear and convincing evidence of the patient's intent and will enforce its provisions. Consult the sources that have been listed for up-to-date verification.

CHAPTER 4

Cruzan and Other Important Cases

In the last decade, public awareness of the right to die has prompted legislatures in all of the states to take some position on the issue (see maps in previous chapter.) What the state laws did not address, the courts did, and although there is still a lot to be resolved in this ever-emerging field of legal discussion, there have been significant decisions that indicate how the courts are reacting to specific questions.

There are many such cases. We will discuss three of them that are important because they define the rights of the parties involved.

Cruzan v. Director of Missouri Department of Health

The *Cruzan* case hit a public nerve. Decided in 1990 by the United States Supreme Court, the case generated publicity that in turn caused a public awareness of the right to die. Congress reacted almost immediately by passing the Patient Self Determination Act, a federal law everyone should be acquainted with that will be discussed later. It is important to understand, however, what the *Cruzan* case held and what it did not.

On January 11, 1983, Nancy Beth Cruzan, then twenty-five, was found unconscious near her overturned car. Paramedics tried to revive her and transported her to Freeman Hospital in Joplin, Missouri. She was diagnosed as having a lacerated liver and probable cerebral contusion compounded by anoxia (deprivation of oxygen). It was estimated that the anoxia had lasted at least twelve minutes, creating her vegetative state.

A gastrostomy tube was implanted on February 7, and rehabilitation efforts were begun, but her condition was unchanged. Her parents were then informed that in theory she could remain in that vegetative state for thirty years. Her parents then asked the hospital employees to end her gastrostomy feeding—a step that would have resulted in her death. The hospital refused.

The Cruzans then sued to compel the hospital to comply with their request. The Missouri Trial Court sided with her parents. It found that there was evidence that strongly suggested that Ms. Cruzan "would not wish to continue with nutrition and hydration" and that she had a "right to liberty." The court then added a dimension that insured its journey to the United States Supreme Court; it held that to deny her co-guardians authority to act on their daughter's behalf would deprive Nancy of *equal protection of the law.*

The hospital successfully appealed. The Missouri Supreme Court, in a 4–3 decision, reversed the lower court. Missouri law required "reliable and strong" evidence that Nancy sought to end her life. The majority of the appellate judges then held that the evidence submitted at the trial court did not reach that level.

It was another close one in the United States Supreme Court. By a 5–4 vote, the majority held that the Court would not interfere with Missouri's laws requiring its higher standard of proof. However, having said that, the Court did acknowledge that there was a Constitutional right to end life, as long as clear and convincing evidence of the patient's intentions is submitted.

One thing was clear. The Supreme Court was not impressed by the words used by the Missouri court when it said that Nancy's parents were asking "to allow the medical profession to make Nancy die by starvation and dehydration."

The four justices who dissented took the position that the State of Missouri, by placing unreasonable obstacles in her parents' path, interfered and deprived Nancy of her fundamental right "to be free of unwanted artificial nutrition and hydration."

In other words, the Supreme Court sent mixed signals in the *Cruzan* case. On one hand it reaffirmed its position taken in earlier decisions, where it found that freedom of choice between life and death is a right protected by the Constitution. But it also held that a state may impose its own standards of proof as to how and in what manner the individual must express his or her intentions before that choice is made by someone else. It came down to matter of proof, and the Court said that a state has a right to set down the rules of proof required as long as they are within reasonable limits. Five judges of the Court felt that Missouri's standards were reasonable—four didn't. Not exactly a clear mandate!

The majority of the judges left no doubt that they would have gone along with the parents' request had Nancy previously expressed her intent to terminate her life if she ever arrived at that incompetent state. But the minority focused on the catch-22 situation. Clearly, a vibrant and healthy twenty-five year old does not anticipate sudden and total loss of mental competence through an accident, and it is therefore unlikely that she would discuss with anyone how she should die if that should occur.

Justice Brennan, in his dissent, stated that the Court could have very well inferred her intent when he described her condition:

> Nancy Cruzan is oblivious to her surroundings and will remain so. Her body twitches only reflexively, without consciousness. The areas of her brain that once thought, felt, and experienced sensations have degenerated badly and are continuing to do so. . . . Nancy will never interact meaningfully with her environment again. She will remain in a persistent vegetative state until her death.*

Professor Louis Michael Seidman of Georgetown Law School, in an article on the *Cruzan* case, writes:

---

*The Supreme Court in effect sent the case back to the Missouri court, who found that there was clear and convincing evidence. As a result, Nancy Cruzan was permitted to die in December, 1990.

The dissent is on solid ground in believing that many people, rightly or wrongly, feel that they are somehow connected to the entity they become when they lose consciousnesss. And there can be no doubt that many people, while conscious, care deeply about what will happen to their loved ones after they are no longer conscious, and indeed, after they are no longer alive. (*Supreme Court Review*, 1991)

The *Cruzan* case served its purpose. Reaction was swift. Congress passed the Patient's Civil Rights Act, officially known as the Patient Self Determination Act, and the individual states through legislation and court decisions, made it easier for those who were placed in that unfortunate position to exercise their freedom of choice. The state courts and legislatures are tending to adopt the philosophy of the dissent, so clearly worded by Justice Brennan:

The right to be free from unwanted medical attention is a right to evaluate the potential benefit of treatment and its possible consequences according to one's own values and to make a personal decision as to whether to subject oneself to the intrusion.

By 1993, nineteen states had passed amendments and/or statutes that have simplified the legal framework and have enhanced awareness of patients' options. They have also permitted an expansion of the scope of advance directives (living wills and health care proxies). A call to the American Bar Association (202-331-2200) or to any of the facilities previously listed in your region, or to your local state bar association (see directory at end of chapter), will provide you with the latest changes in your state's laws and also with its current court decisions.

As an example of this trend, let us return to the Supreme Court of Missouri, and see how the court, and the state, changed its thinking. The *Busalacchi* case was decided on January 26, 1993—three years after the Supreme Court decided *Cruzan*.

The Busalacchi Case

On May 29, 1987, Christine Busalacchi, then seventeen, suffered serious injuries as a result of an automobile accident. A large portion of her brain was removed. A gastrostomy tube was inserted in her stomach to provide her with nutrition and hydration. Christine was in the same condition as Nancy Cruzan had been—a persistent vegetative state.

In December 1990, Christine's father, Peter Busalacchi, feeling that Christine and the family had suffered enough, attempted to move Christine to a facility outside Missouri, where her feeding tube could legally be removed. The Missouri Rehabilitation Center—the state facility where she had been housed—objected to the move, as did the Missouri Department of Health. Both joined in a legal action to prevent Christine's transfer.

The trial court found in favor of Peter Busalacchi. It set forth three grounds for doing so.

First: The law in Missouri did not prevent a father from moving his daughter to another state.

Second: Christine was entitled to the laws of other states under the Constitution's full faith and credit provision.

Third: A minor's physician and family is in the best position to determine what constitutes appropriate medical treatment.

The Missouri Department of Health appealed, claiming, as Missouri did in the *Cruzan* case, that the court did not have clear and convincing evidence that Christine would choose to discontinue tube feeding. The Missouri Supreme Court, who seemed to have a problem with the entire concept of choice, sent it back to the trial court to determine whether she was in fact in a persistent vegetative state.

To the credit of the trial court, it again found that her condition was, as it was before, a persistent vegetative state. The court further found that her condition was permanent and that there was no chance of significant improvement. The trial court then denied the request of the health department to declare Christine a "developmentally disabled person" entitled to special legal protection. The court saw this maneuver for what it was —a delaying tactic. The request was denied as was the additional request that the father be denied authority to discontinue tube feedings.

But that didn't end it. Attorney General Webster of Missouri *again* appealed to the Missouri Supreme Court. If Peter Busalacchi had prayed to end this ordeal, his prayers were answered in a most practical fashion, because before the appeal could be heard, the voters of

Missouri elected a new attorney general, Jay Nixon, who apparently had had enough of the state's interference in the Busalacchi family's ordeal. He petitioned the Missouri Supreme Court to dismiss the appeal voluntarily. The motion was granted, and the appeal was dismissed. The feeding tube was removed.

Belcher v. Charleston Area Medical Center

In the *Belcher* case, the shoe was on the other foot. Freedom of choice was denied the patient, and unfortunately, the medical authorities prevailed upon the parents to make the decision that he should have been given the opportunity to make.

Larry Belcher was afflicted with muscular dystrophy and was confined to a wheelchair. On December 19, 1986, Larry was rushed to the Charleston Area Medical Center in Charleston, West Virginia. He had stopped breathing after choking on his own mucus. At the time, Larry was seventeen years and eight months old.

He had a second episode after his admission and was placed on a ventilator. A few days later he recovered sufficiently to have the respirator removed. However, the attending physician informed the parents that Larry would probably go into respiratory arrest again.

The doctor then asked the parents if they wished to sign a do not resuscitate (DNR) order. They eventually agreed, without consulting Larry, that he should not be placed on the ventilator again. Larry died on December 24, after going into respiratory arrest. This time the hospital staff took no steps to resuscitate him.

Larry's parents sued the hospital for malpractice, alleging that Larry should have been consulted before an official DNR order was issued. The jury found for the hospital, and the parents appealed.

The West Virginia Supreme Court of Appeals reversed the jury's verdict and sent the case back to the West Virginia trial court to determine whether Larry was sufficiently mature to give his consent before the treatment was withheld. In its decision, the appeals court refused to set a specific age at which a minor would be considered mature enough to consent, or refuse to consent, to medical treatment. Instead, the court held that whether a minor is mature is a question that should be determined by several factors, i.e., age, ability, experience, education, training, and "capacity to appreciate the nature, risk, and consequences of the medical procedure to be performed, or the treatment to be administered or withheld."

The court observed:

> It is difficult to imagine that a young person who is under the age of majority, yet, who has undergone medical treatment for a permanent or recurring illness over the course of a long period of time, may not be capable of taking part in decisions concerning that treatment.

In deciding the *Belcher* case, the court added West Virginia to the many states that have adopted the "mature minor" rule. One of the basic principles of the common law that we inherited from the English is that the parents or guardians of "minors" have the right to make vital decisions on their behalf and that the law must recognize that right.

There has now developed an exception to that rule. The "mature minor" concept, adopted by West Virginia and other states, stands for the proposition that age alone is not the sole determining factor as to whether a minor may make a decision concerning his or her welfare. It is the maturity of the individual that is of equal importance—the ability to appreciate risks and benefits of a medical procedure and the ability to make an intelligent choice.

The cases emphasize that young people should seriously consider executing advance written directives. If a cruel fate decrees that one should find himself or herself in a situation similar to Nancy Cruzan or Christine Busalacchi, the written instrument would have to be given substantial weight when the issue of accepting or declining medical treatment arose. This is true especially if the patient is incompetent.

The document may not be legally binding (in the event that the patient is a minor) but in states like West Virginia, which have adopted the "mature minor" rule, the document would be strong evidence of the patient's intent and, if voluntarily and understandably executed, would be enforced.

Legislatures pass laws, but the courts interpret them. The Supreme Court decided in the *Cruzan* case that the right of an individual to choose how to die does exist, but individual states have the right to set the rules as to how that right is to be administered.

The national trend of court decisions—both state and federal—has been to make it easier for the patient or the health care agent to make that choice and to carry out the wishes of that patient. Nevertheless, the decisions vary from state to state, and it is important that you be informed about your particular state's current decisions on all phases of the laws applying to the choice in dying.

The following list of state bar associations includes addresses and phone numbers making it easy for you to obtain immediate information.

State Bar Directory

ALABAMA STATE BAR
ASSOCIATION
P.O. Box 671
Montgomery, AL 36101
800-392-5660

ALASKA STATE BAR
ASSOCIATION
P.O. Box 100279
Anchorage, AK 99510
907-272-0352

STATE BAR OF ARIZONA
333 West Roosevelt
Phoenix, AZ 85003
602-257-4434

ARKANSAS STATE
BAR ASSOCIATION
400 West Markham
Little Rock, AR 72201
501-375-4605

STATE BAR OF CALIFORNIA
555 Franklin Street
San Francisco, CA 94102
415-561-8200

COLORADO STATE
BAR ASSOCIATION
1301 Pennsylvania Street
Suite 450
Denver, CO 80203
303-831-8000

CONNECTICUT STATE
BAR ASSOCIATION
61 Hungerford Street
Hartford, CT 06106
203-525-6052

DISTRICT OF COLUMBIA
BAR
Suite 600
1707 L Street NW
Washington, DC 20036
202-331-3883

DELAWARE STATE
BAR ASSOCIATION
708 Market Street Mall
820 North French Street
Wilmington, DE 19801
302-658-5278

THE FLORIDA STATE
BAR ASSOCIATION
The Florida Bar Center
Tallahassee, FL 32399-2300
904-561-5600

STATE BAR OF GEORGIA
800 The Hurt Building
50 Hurt Plaza
Atlanta, GA 30303
404-527-8700

HAWAII STATE
BAR ASSOCIATION
P.O. Box 26
Honolulu, HI 96810
808-537-9140

IDAHO STATE
BAR ASSOCIATION
P.O. Box 895
Boise, ID 83701
208-342-8958

ILLINOIS STATE
BAR ASSOCIATION
Illinois Bar Center
Springfield, IL 62701
217-525-1760

INDIANA STATE
BAR ASSOCIATION
230 East Ohio
4th Floor
Indianapolis, IN 46204
317-639-5465

IOWA STATE
BAR ASSOCIATION
1101 Fleming Building
Des Moines, IA 50309
515-243-3179

KANSAS STATE
BAR ASSOCIATION
712 S.W. Kansas Avenue
2nd Floor
Topeka, KS 66603
913-233-4322

KENTUCKY STATE
BAR ASSOCIATION
West Main at Kentucky River
Frankfort, KY 40601
502-564-3795

LOUISIANA STATE
BAR ASSOCIATION
210 O'Keefe Avenue
Suite 600
New Orleans, LA 70112
504-561-8828

MAINE STATE
BAR ASSOCIATION
124 State Street
P.O. Box 788
Augusta, ME 04330
207-622-7523

MARYLAND STATE
BAR ASSOCIATION
520 West Sayette Street
Baltimore, MD 21201
301-685-7878

MASSACHUSETTS STATE
BAR ASSOCIATION
20 West Street
Boston, MA 02111
617-542-9103

STATE BAR OF MICHIGAN
306 Townsend Street
Lansing, MI 48933
517-372-9030

MINNESOTA STATE
BAR ASSOCIATION
430 Marquette Avenue
Suite 403
Minneapolis, MN 55401
612-333-1183

MISSISSIPPI STATE
BAR ASSOCIATION
P.O. Box 2168
Jackson, MS 39225-2168
601-948-5488

THE MISSOURI BAR
ASSOCIATION
P.O. Box 119
Jefferson City, MO 65102
314-635-4128

STATE BAR OF MONTANA
P.O. Box 577
Helena, MT 59624
406-499-6577

NEBRASKA STATE
BAR ASSOCIATION
635 S. 14th Street
Lincoln, NE 68508
402-475-7091

NEW HAMPSHIRE STATE
BAR ASSOCIATION
18 Centre Street
Concord, NH 03301
603-224-6934

NEW JERSEY STATE
BAR ASSOCIATION
1530 Brunswick Avenue
Suite 204
Lawrenceville, NJ 08648
609-989-8880

STATE BAR OF NEW
MEXICO
P.O. Box 25883
Albuquerque, NM 87125
505-842-6132

NEW YORK STATE BAR
ASSOCIATION
One Elk Street
Albany, NY 12207
518-463-3200

NORTH CAROLINA STATE
BAR ASSOCIATION
1312 Annapolis Drive
Raleigh, NC 27605
919-828-1054

STATE BAR ASSOCIATION
OF NORTH DAKOTA
P.O. Box 2136
Bismarck, ND 58502
701-255-1406

OHIO STATE BAR
ASSOCIATION
40 South Third Street
6th Floor
Columbus, OH 43215
614-221-0754

OREGON STATE
BAR ASSOCIATION
5200 SW Meadows Road
Lake Oswego, OR 97035
800-452-8260

OKLAHOMA STATE
BAR ASSOCIATION
P.O. Box 53036
Oklahoma City, OK 73152
405-524-2365

PENNSYLVANIA STATE
BAR ASSOCIATION
100 South Street
P.O. Box 186
Harrisburg, PA 17108
717-238-6715

PUERTO RICAN STATE
BAR ASSOCIATION
P.O. Box 1900
San Juan, PR 09003
809-724-3358

RHODE ISLAND STATE
BAR ASSOCIATION
91 Friendship Street
Providence, RI 02903
401-421-7799

SOUTH CAROLINA
STATE BAR
950 Taylor Street
Columbia, SC 29201
803-799-7100

STATE BAR OF
SOUTH DAKOTA
222 East Capitol
Pierre, SD 57501
605-224-7554

TENNESSEE STATE
BAR ASSOCIATION
3622 West End Avenue
Nashville, TN 37205
615-383-7421

STATE BAR OF TEXAS
P.O. Box 12487
Capital Station
Austin, TX 78711
512-463-1463

UTAH STATE BAR
ASSOCIATION
645 South 200 East
Salt Lake City, UT 84111
801-531-9075

VERMONT STATE BAR
ASSOCIATION
P.O. Box 100
Montpelier, VT 05602
800-642-3153

VIRGINIA STATE
BAR ASSOCIATION
801 East Main Street
10th floor
Richmond, VA 23219
804-786-5966

WASHINGTON STATE
BAR ASSOCIATION
10020 A Main Street
Suite 500
Bellevue, WA 98004
206-235-8110

WEST VIRGINIA STATE
BAR ASSOCIATION
P.O. Box 346
Charleston, WV 25322
304-257-4666

WYOMING STATE
BAR ASSOCIATION
P.O. Box 109
Cheyenne, WY 82001
307-632-9061

CHAPTER 5

Your Rights Under the Patient Self Determination Act

Since 1976, there have been several cases that have alerted the American public to a right not contemplated by our founding fathers. We are all familiar with "life, liberty, and the pursuit of happiness." But the right to choose to die with peace and dignity was not considered—or even contemplated two hundred years ago.

After the *Cruzan* case was decided, the attendant publicity caused a groundswell that moved Congress, in 1990, to pass the Patient Self Determination Act. Basically, the law required that every hospital and nursing home provide information about patient rights. Actually, all health institutions caring for patients came under that mandate. Not only were they required to inform patients upon admission about their rights to express advance directives (living will, health proxy, and even oral declarations), but in addition those institutions were compelled to develop policies about these directives. In other words, the subject was to have been

61

made highly visible—inviting and leading to more discussions about options at the end of life that could be openly discussed between families and physicians.

All of the fifty states have either passed similar legislation conforming with the act, or have had court decisions that do the same. It is safe to say that every hospital, nursing home, or other health institution has been alerted to federal and/or state regulations requiring the education of patients as to their rights of self-determination regarding the continuance or cessation of life-sustaining procedures.

Each state has its own particular requirements, but they all trace the federal law requiring all adults on admission to be provided with written information about their rights under the law. Generally, the following information *must* be furnished:

1. A description of the law that summarizes the rights, duties, and requirements relating to orders not to resuscitate. It must state and define the right of an adult (as your state court defines an adult) to give attending medical personnel instructions about treatment in advance.

2. The institution must note in your medical record your advance directive if in fact you made one.

3. A summary of the facility's or agency's policy regarding the implementation of these rights.

4. The institution may not discriminate against you because you have issued an advance directive.

5. The institution will provide staff and community education on advance directives. In this context, "staff" in-

cludes all those who provide patient care or otherwise regularly interact with patients.

6. The institution must partake in community education concerning advance directives with respect to providers participating in Medicaid and Medicare programs.

7. Medical providers will inform both inpatients *and* outpatients about advance directives.

The law requires that advance directive information be posted in a public place. Nursing homes must educate residents concerning health care proxies to ensure that each resident who creates a proxy while residing in the facility has done so voluntarily. Nursing homes must designate one or more individuals to respond to questions and assist residents with respect to advance directives.

It cannot be said too often that general instructions about refusing treatment, even if written, may not be effective. The Patient Self Determination Act does not include provisions for compelling the doctor to guess your intention. For example, if you have only written that you do not want "heroic measures," as a patient did in one case, the doctor may refuse to honor the wish because the instruction is too vague, and if your physician has to interpret your instructions, he'd be within his rights to refuse to follow them.

When you draw up your health care proxy or living will, be completely informed. This may very well be the most important document that you will ever sign. Consult your physician, especially when he or she has knowledge of your medical history, and ask her or him to suggest the specific recommendations he or she would make as to what to include in the directive.

It is almost certain that your physician will make reference to cardiopulmonary resuscitation (CPR). As previously explained, CPR is emergency treatment to restart the heart and/or lungs when your breathing or circulation stops. Sometimes doctors and patients decide in advance that CPR should not be provided. If there is such an agreement, the doctor gives the medical staff the order: do not resuscitate (DNR). If your physical or mental condition is such that you are capable of entering into such an agreement, there is no problem. But if you are not capable, the court decisions clearly hold that in most instances, a proxy, named in an advance document, would be required to make that decision for you. But it is not wise to restrict the powers of your health care proxy to CPR or DNR. If you should become incompetent, it would make sense for your agent to be empowered to make *all* health care decisions for you. You have placed your trust in that person, and he or she should be empowered without restriction to act in your behalf.

The acceptance of the right to refuse medical treatment by national and state courts is no longer in doubt. But what happens when your specific direction, or that of your loved one, is not followed by either the doctor or the hospital, or both?

As this is written, legal actions are being brought throughout the nation seeking compensation for having those orders ignored. It is going to be increasingly difficult for medical providers to disregard advance directives that are specific and clear. Remember that the Patient Self Determination Act now requires every health care institution to have an "active" policy that will inform patients of these rights. As a result of this education, public consciousness about the entire concept of choice in dying will be raised, leading to the existence of more and more written advance directives.

There is an evolving field of law that defines the legal remedies available to patients, and/or their families, whose right to choose was violated. Let us examine some of these cases, keeping in mind that we are just scratching the surface.

Leach v. Shapiro

The Ohio case of *Leach v. Shapiro* was brought on the basis that unwanted intrusion into the human body is an assault and battery. Actually, the legal theory is not new. Justice Benjamin Cardozo, in 1914, wrote:

> Every human being of adult years and sound mind has a right to determine what shall be done with his own body—and a surgeon who performs an operation without his patient's consent commits an assault for which he is liable in damages.

Justice Cardozo was way ahead of his time. It took seventy years to develop the battery theory into a significant lawsuit for civil damages. There have been many since Leach, but the Leach case is important because it is the first major litigation to present the battery concept.

Edna Marie Leach suffered a respiratory failure. After entering the hospital she went into cardiac arrest. She responded to resuscitation, but then regressed and entered into a chronic vegetative state. She was eventually placed on life support.

It was alleged in the court papers that placing her on life support was done without her consent and contrary to her expressed wishes, which were clearly stated while she was still competent. The hospital refused to discontinue the procedure. Her husband finally obtained a court order allowing the treatment to be terminated.

Her family brought an action for damages claiming battery. The lower court dismissed the complaint. Upon appeal, the complaint was reinstated. The Ohio Appellate Court held that the lower court was in error in not allowing the case to go to trial, to decide whether Edna had expressly refused to consent to life support, whether the hospital and physicians had ignored that request, and whether her family was adequately informed of her condition and treatment. The case was then remanded (returned to) the trial court, where the hospital promptly settled for $50,000.

The *Leach* case is important because it puts hospitals and physicians on notice that the clear and explicit directives by an individual about his or her treatment may not be ignored. It recognizes an individual's right to choose the treatment he or she will receive and mandates that the introduction of tubes or other apparatuses into the human body without consent and over objection is a violation of that right. It is in fact an unwarranted assault that if done with reckless disregard for the expressed intent of the patient can result in liability for substantial damages.

The Ohio court also recognized that a patient can be intimidated by the awesome atmosphere of the hospital, where the patient and family are so vulnerable to suggestion and persuasion. Nevertheless, while in the care and custody of that institution, medical personnel may not disregard specific declared intentions about what is to be done with a patient.

Westhart v. Mule

The California case of *Westhart v. Mule* addresses the issue of infliction of emotional distress to the family when the loved one is kept alive for no apparent reason. The theory is that when this is done, the family suffers a wrong for which they should be compensated.

Intentional infliction of emotional distress is not an easy case to prove. You have to show that the conduct of the hospital was "extreme and outrageous."

There is an old adage that states that bad cases make bad law. Despite the emotional distress of the seventy-one-year-old incompetent's wife, who brought the action, the hard fact is that the case should never have begun in the first place. She had initially refused to consent to the insertion of a feeding tube, but eventually relented. Seven months after her husband's death, she sued upon learning that the feeding tube was a form of life support that she could have refused, in compliance with her husband's wishes. She claimed that the doctors knew, or should have known, that prolonging her husband's death would cause her emotional distress.

Unfortunately, although the theory is an accepted one, the facts of this particular case were not persuasive and the judge dismissed the complaint for good reason. The wife had never asked to have the feeding tube removed. Also, the doctors were never given the opportunity to either accede to the patient's wishes or transfer him to another institution that would.

But let's change the facts a bit. Let us assume a different set of circumstances, where the wife had made a specific request to remove the feeding tube, the doctors had a reasonable opportunity to comply, but they nevertheless refused. That scenario could lead a jury to find that the physicians, "knew or should have known that she would have suffered emotional distress."

While emotional distress cases are difficult to prove, they are not impossible. Under the proper set of facts— where the physicians were directly instructed and had ample opportunity to abide with those instructions but refused to do so—a substantial verdict could result in the plaintiff's favor.

There is still another factor that the hospitals should take into consideration before they impose treatment over the objection of the patient. Currently, there are a line of cases that indicate that such conduct could be expensive.

In a Rhode Island case, a fee of more than $38,000 was awarded to an attorney who was successful in obtaining an order from the court directing that a feeding tube be removed from a woman in a persistent vegetative state. The hospital involved could have saved themselves that small bundle if they had complied with the request of the family and had not compelled the hiring of a lawyer to make them do what they were legally obliged to do in the first place. The same thing happened in California, only more so, where a court granted more than $160,000 in court costs and attorney's fees.

These decisions should act as a realistic and practical deterrent to the wanton disregard of patient's rights as they are defined under the Patient Self Determination Act. It can be safely assumed that attorneys for hospitals and other health care institutions have informed their clients that the trend of decisions seems to favor patients' rights—and that there better be firm ground for forcing on those patients unauthorized and unwanted life-support systems.

It would be especially prudent for health-care institutions to be aware of a New York case decided in favor of the patient's family. It is equally important that all who may enter a hospital at some time in their lives (meaning everybody) acquaint themselves with the court decision as well. The facts of the *Elbaum* case are a classic example of circumstances that point to the "clear and convincing evidence" needed to prove the patient's intent. But this case, as the *Cruzan* case, sent a mixed message. Apparently defying logic, the appeals court held that the patient's family was liable for medical costs, even though instructions to refuse treatment were ignored.

Elbaum v. Grace Plaza

On June 30, 1986, Jean Elbaum entered North Shore
University Hospital suffering from headaches, memory
difficulties, and confusion. During the next thirty to
forty hours, her condition deteriorated and she lapsed
into a coma. Her physician then directed the use of a
nasogastric tube (a device that is inserted through the
nose and into the stomach to provide nutrition and hydration). On July 28, she was diagnosed as being in an
"irreversible, persistent, vegetative state with no hope of
recovery."

When the Elbaum family was notified of her condition, they were also told that a surgical procedure called
a gastrostomy was necessary to keep her alive, surgery
involving the insertion of a feeding tube through the
abdominal wall. The family was informed that Mrs. Elbaum would require long-term nursing care and that no
nursing home would accept her as a patient without her
first having a gastrostomy.

From the very outset, the family resisted the gastrostomy. Her husband asked what would happen if he refused to give his consent to the procedure. The physician responded that the hospital would be required to
institute legal proceedings to authorize the surgical procedure.*

Nevertheless, the family hesitated. Her husband told

---

*The New York Appellate Court later made reference to the fact
that when the eventual consent was made under threat of legal

the physician that the Elbaum family was reluctant to consent to the insertion of the gastrointestinal tube in view of Mrs. Elbaum's previously stated wish to the contrary. In testimony at the trial, the attending physician admitted that the Elbaum family continued to "drag their feet and be extremely reluctant to sign for the gastrostomy."

The family was repeatedly threatened with legal proceedings unless they gave their consent. Finally, the family was worn down, and on September 2, 1986, the gastrostomy was performed. Two weeks later, Mrs. Elbaum was transferred to Grace Plaza, the defendant nursing home.

On the eve of the transfer to the nursing home, Mr. Elbaum and his daughter met with Dr. Lester Corn, the medical director of Grace Plaza. According to their testimony at the hearing, the family advised the director that Jean Elbaum had previously stated that in the event that she was ever in a "vegetable-like" state, with no hope of recovery, she would not want to be kept alive. They further testified that she specifically stated that she did not want the use of a respirator, antibiotics, or tubes to keep her alive.

Shortly after Mrs. Elbaum's arrival at the Grace Plaza Nursing Home, Mr. Elbaum, by letter dated September 22, 1986, provided the home with a do not resuscitate (DNR) order whereby it was advised that his wife was to receive no resuscitation and no heroic measures were to be taken to sustain her life. The order further provided

proceedings, such consent did not constitute a voluntary act fatal to the plaintiff's case.

that in the event Mrs. Elbaum developed an infection, no antibiotics or drug treatments were to be administered, and that no mechanical or artificial respiratory means were to be taken to sustain her life.

After Mr. Elbaum provided Grace Plaza with the DNR order he repeatedly advised Dr. Corn, *on at least six to twelve different occasions,* of his wife's wishes with respect to the nonuse of respirators, tubes, and antibiotics. The doctor was also advised that Mrs. Elbaum had expressly stated, on several occasions, that she would not want the use of feeding tubes if she were in an irreversible vegetative state. According to Elbaum, these discussions occurred because the nursing home continued to administer antibiotics without Elbaum's knowledge and consent, and in complete disregard to his prior, clearly stated instructions.

Dr. Corn admitted that he never notified the Elbaum family that he had administered antibiotics to Mrs. Elbaum in 1987. He stated, however, that these treatments were necessary to prevent the possibility of infection to the other patients. Why the Elbaum family was not informed of this was left unexplained.

Then, on October 6, 1987, Mr. Elbaum sent letters to Dr. Corn and Celia Strow, the administrator of Grace Plaza, requesting that, in keeping with his wife's previously described wishes, the nursing home and its staff "refrain from administering anything other than comfort care to her."

On October 9, 1987, Dr. Corn responded to Mr. Elbaum's request by stating that the withdrawal of the gastrointestinal tube was contrary to the "dedication to the law, and to the policies and the philosophy of Grace

Plaza." After receiving that letter, Mr. Elbaum ceased making all payments to Grace Plaza for his wife's care.

Celia Strow, the administrator of Grace Plaza, testified at the trial that after her receipt of Mr. Elbaum's letter of October 6, 1987, in which he requested the removal of his wife's gastrointestinal tube, she had a conversation with Mr. Elbaum. She said that she informed him of the facility's policy against such an action and that she thereafter attempted to find a suitable nursing facility that would agree to it.

In a letter dated February 16, 1988, she advised Elbaum that the search for a transfer sight had been unsuccessful. Then she made a very interesting declaration. She wrote that the nursing home did not have a clear indication of Mrs. Elbaum's wishes (despite the overwhelming evidence of notice). But she went further. Quoting from the hearing record, she wrote *"even if irrefutable evidence"* was forthcoming establishing that Mrs. Elbaum would want the gastrointestinal tube removed, the nursing home would not remove it. In the same letter, Ms. Strow notified Elbaum that he was presently in arrears in the sum of approximately $18,500 in medical payments for his wife's care and that unless payment thereof was received, legal proceedings for payment would be instituted.

At that point, the family had had it. In June 1988, Mr. Elbaum, as his wife's conservator, brought an action on his wife's behalf requesting the court to order that Grace Plaza and Dr. Corn refrain from providing nutrition or hydration to Mrs. Elbaum through any mechanical means. He also asked that the court order them to stop providing *any* further life-sustaining treatment.

The testimony at the hearing for this injunction was overwhelming in establishing the "clear and convincing" evidence of Mrs. Elbaum's wishes. Unlike the California case previously cited *(Westhart v. Mule)*, where the evidence was vague and uncertain, this testimony should have been clear to the judge.

Mr. Elbaum was the first witness. He testified that he had been married to Mrs. Elbaum for over thirty-six years and that his wife had first expressed her views on extraordinary or life-sustaining treatment in discussing the Karen Ann Quinlan case and viewing the story of her family's torture. At the time, Mrs. Elbaum remarked, "How awful it must be for the parents to sit vigil over a virtually dead or comatose daughter," and that if she, Mrs. Elbaum, were in a similar situation, "she would not want to be on any other mechanical means, she wanted to die."

Elbaum further testified that his wife remarked about another well-publicized case—Sunny Von Bulow. Mrs. Elbaum expressed an inability to comprehend how the Von Bulow family could permit Mrs. Von Bulow to be sustained as a "vegetable," and she added, "I do not want to be sustained as a vegetable, I want to die with some dignity."

There was still a third occasion where Mrs. Elbaum expressed her views on the subject. Elbaum testified that in 1982 a family friend suffered a stroke and was rendered unconscious while riding in the Elbaum's car. They took the friend to a nearby hospital at which time they were informed that the friend was comatose. Later, while the Elbaums were returning home from the hospital, Mrs. Elbaum told her husband, "Murray, I want you to tell me now, I am telling you and I want you to tell me that you will not do anything to sustain my life in the event that I am a vegetable." In discussing the incident again, she said, "If I am ever in a similar state and it is hopeless, I don't want to be sustained by any tubes or machines or antibiotics."

The next witness to testify was Renee Schutzer, Mrs. Elbaum's sister. She too had several conversations with her sister concerning the Karen Ann Quinlan and Sonny Von Bulow cases. Mrs. Schutzer testified that on another occasion Mrs. Elbaum, after viewing the film *Whose Life is it Anyway,* which involved the right of an incapacitated person to refuse medical treatment, described it as a "horrible situation" that was "very disturbing to her."

Mrs. Schutzer then referred to the experience of their mother, who was terminally ill with cancer, being fed through a nasogastric feeding tube. She said that Mrs. Elbaum became "very adamant about pledging to me and asking me to pledge to her that these measures would not be administered to her or me if there was no hope of recovery." On many occasions after their mother's death, the sisters expressed regret at permitting the use of forced feeding, respiratory assistance, and medication on their mother. Thereafter, the sisters "made a pledge to one another not to permit it to be done with no hope of recovery." That pledge was reiterated at the unveiling of the mother's tombstone, when they again discussed "where (they) had gone wrong in handling (their) mother's death" and promised each other that "if it was within our power we would not permit those life-prolonging measures if there was no hope."

Mrs. Elbaum's son, Joshua, testified next. He also referred to his mother's agreement with the decision made by Karen Ann Quinlan's parents to disconnect their daughter from a respirator and to her support for the position of refusing medical treatment as shown in *Whose Life Is It Anyway*. Similarly, Joshua stated that his mother was shaken by the manner in which his grandmother died and indicated to him that she did not want "to die a slow, lingering death like her mother did." He then repeated her request that if she were ever in a comalike state, he and his sister should do everything they could not to maintain her, since she believed there was no sense to that type of existence.

Finally, Mrs. Elbaum's daughter, Anne, testified that on one occasion after she and her mother had visited her grandmother, Mrs. Elbaum told her about the effect the sight of the nasogastric tube inserted in her mother had on her—that she had "nightmares about it" and "couldn't get it out of her head."

Decision of the Lower Court

Despite the overwhelming evidence elicited at the hearing, the lower court came to an amazing and incomprehensible conclusion. It determined that insufficient evidence had been adduced to establish by clear and convincing proof that Mrs. Elbaum, while competent, made a firm decision that she would not want the use of a feeding tube to keep her alive if she were in a a persistent vegetative state with no hope of recovery. And in a further mind-boggling conclusion, the court held that Mrs. Elbaum's statements concerning the use of artificial and extraordinary means to prolong life (which were described so unequivocably by her husband, sister, and children) were *merely emotional responses to unsettling events and were not contemplative in nature.*

The court further stated that it denied the application because of the *absence of any evidence indicating that Mrs. Elbaum, while competent, had specifically contemplated death by starvation or dehydration or was familiar with the consequences thereof.** The court concluded that the state's interest in preserving the integrity of the medical profession outweighed Mrs. Elbaum's interest since Grace Plaza and its staff would be required to perform a morally objectionable act.

The lower court, for the reasons stated, dismissed the Elbaum's complaint and found for the nursing home. The effect of that decision was that Mrs. Elbaum would remain in a vegetative state indefinitely until she was fortunate enough to die.

Decision of the Appellate Court

The appellate court, applying common sense as well as the law, reversed the lower court decision and granted the injunction sought by the Elbaums. It ordered Grace

---

* I have added the emphasis to indicate how the conclusion of the court varied from the evidence presented.

Plaza to either transfer Mrs. Elbaum to a facility that
would remove the gastrointestinal tube, or assist the
Elbaums to remove it, or to permit a physician selected
by the family to enter the facility for that purpose. The
court completely disagreed with the lower court in its
interpretation of Mrs. Elbaum's intent. It found, based
upon the evidence, that her repeated extractions of a
series of promises from her family reflected a "serious
and consistent purpose of mind and intent to bind others to effectuate her desire" in the future. The court
took note, as the lower court should have, of her constant references to "hopeless circumstances" and her
fear of becoming a "vegetable." It identified her reflec-
tions on the subject of artificial and extraordinary medical treatments as "solemn pronouncements."

In addition, the appeals court dealt with the insensitive reference that Grace Plaza made to Mr. Elbaum's
motive in instructing them to discontinue treatment.

> We reject the assertion that Mr. Elbaum was moti-
> vated solely by economic factors when he served his
> October 1987 letters on the defendants and directed
> the removal of Mrs. Elbaum's gastrointestinal tube.
> Rather, we view Mr. Elbaum's letters and his subsequent
> cessation of payments as a protest against the defen-
> dant's disregard for his DNR (do not resuscitate) order
> and their continued use of a gastrointestinal feeding
> tube over his objection.

One can reasonably conclude that the appeals court
harbored some question about the nursing home's motive when the court found:

The evidence reflects that despite the receipt of Mr. Elbaum's DNR order and despite complaints concerning the administration of antibiotics and the use of feeding tubes on his wife, the defendants ignored Mr. Elbaum's demands *while simultaneously insisting upon payment for undesired services.* (emphasis added)

The court added that this was not a "substituted judgment" case, where Mr. Elbaum was substituting his judgment for his wife. That he supplied the DNR order after his wife was not competent to do so did not take away from the evidence, which clearly indicated her feelings while she *was* competent and had an opportunity to make her views known in no uncertain terms.

Additionally, the court addressed the issue that Grace Plaza raised in reference to the nursing home's interest in maintaining its perceived ethical integrity as well as that of the medical profession. This is a defense that some hospitals, nursing homes, and other health care institutions use when all else fails.

The court unequivocably put to rest such questions of morality and medical integrity, in language that should be remembered and referred to if and when the issue is raised.

The interest of maintaining the medical profession's ethical integrity has been overcome, or at least sufficiently lessened, by prevailing ethical standards which do not require medical intervention at all costs. Indeed if the patient's right to informed consent is to have any meaning at all, *it must be accorded respect even when it conflicts with the advice of the doctor or the values of the medical profession as a whole."* (emphasis added)

It was then that the *Elbaum* case took a bizzare turn. The Court of Appeals, New York's highest appellate court, while not disturbing the intermediate appeals court ruling that ordered the nursing home to remove Mrs. Elbaum's feeding tube, nevertheless ruled that Mr. Elbaum was obliged to pay for all services rendered to her after they denied his request to terminate the treatment. This obvious inconsistency was based on prior New York court rulings that right-to-die decisions cannot be made by the family and that "clear and convincing" evidence, as far as New York is concerned, must be in the form of an advance written directive by the patient.

That standard is more stringent than almost any other state's. Twenty-six states have passed laws that give relatives and friends the right to terminate life support for incapacitated persons. Courts in every other state except New York and Missouri have conveyed that right. The obvious reluctance by the New York Court of Appeals to render that decision was evidenced by one of the judges, Stewart F. Hancock, Jr., who called the New York law unworkable and strongly urged that the legislature pass a new law that would allow family members to make right-to-die decisions.

The book is not yet closed on the *Elbaum* case. Elbaum's lawyer, Jody Pope, announced that he would appeal the ruling to the United States Supreme Court arguing that "the sad and unacceptable result of this decision is that patients can be treated against their will and then be made to pay for it, a notion that violates not only the law, but logic and sympathy as well."

It must be repeated that this case would probably be

decided differently in all the other states except New York and Missouri. In most jurisdictions, hospitals and nursing homes have been put on notice through specific state laws and court decisions that they cannot be expected to be paid for unwanted services. There was nothing to indicate that the defendant, Grace Plaza, acted for unethical reasons in the Elbaum case. Yet there are nursing homes and even hospitals for that matter that are motivated by the future collection of substantial medical bills. They cannot hide behind the claim that it is immoral or unethical to recognize and respect the right of an individual and his or her family to terminate the suffering. It is moral and ethical, however, to comply with the individual's wishes. Legislation has been introduced in the New York legislature to adopt the standard of proof accepted by the rest of the country, namely, that the rights of the dying patient can be expressed through his or her loved ones.

Even if the Supreme Court does not reverse the *Elbaum* case, the rest of the states have made their intent clear to the health care industry. They must respect the wishes of the decision maker if he or she presents persuasive evidence, even if not written in advance, that the patient desired to terminate treatment.

Further, the consequences for delaying the termination of life support without good cause could be more costly than just providing services for nothing. State laws vary on the computation of monetary damages, but as the Patient Self Determination Act becomes more visible, abridgment of a patient's rights could result in the payment of substantial damages, including the legal fees involved in litigation.

The New York courts, on the one hand finding that the evidence was sufficient to order the nursing home to terminate treatment but on the other hand ordering Mr. Elbaum to pay for services rendered after that evidence was presented, have created a temporary illogical scenario that, fortunately, the rest of the country does not follow. However, the bright side is that the cases cited where health care providers have resisted the declared intent of the patient's family are the exception, not the rule. The large majority of hospitals and physicians are sensitive to the welfare of their patients—physically, mentally, and emotionally.

Nevertheless, President Clinton had questionable medical costs in mind when on "Meet the Press" (November 7, 1993) he urged families to consider living wills that stipulate when an ailing person should be allowed to die, suggesting "that's one way to weed . . . out" these unnecessary financial burdens that can be imposed on the individuals and on the system.

The real hope is that in time these matters will stay out of the courts entirely. The Patient Self Determination Act has been instrumental in making both patients and health care providers aware of the options that patients have. The present court activity on these questions may be because the effects of the act have not been felt completely. The concept of choice in dying is relatively new, although now recognized, and there is confusion and natural resistance to any change. When the dust settles, and both sides fully comprehend what is legally required, litigation of these issues will be rare. Indeed, the hospitals have in most instances gone along with the urging of the courts that there be private resolutions of these matters. They are forming committees to review requests on treatment termination so as to make fair and objective determinations. Most large hospitals already have that apparatus in place.

No litigation is pleasant, but in cases of this nature it is especially harmful to both sides. For the patient's family, it is costly, time consuming, and can wreck them emotionally. It is to no one's advantage to put families like the Cruzans and the Elbaums through the torturous experience of compounding their sorrows. For the hospital or nursing home, win or lose, they are placed in a negative public-relations position.

It would appear that the safest way to avoid this heartache is through an advance directive. Even the court in the *Elbaum* case indicated that there would have been no payment due to the nursing home for services to Mrs. Elbaum if she had executed a health care proxy or living will, but more important, the family would not have had to bear the anguish of delay before her life-sustaining treatment was stopped.

The happy by-product of the Patient Self Determination Act (PSDA) is the passage of laws by state legislatures throughout the nation that set forth, in "clear and convincing language," the Patient Bill of Rights, a declaration of the rights that the act bestows on all Americans.

The language may differ from state to state, but the basic entitlements are the same. Following are the New York State regulations. They are a guide as to what you are absolutely entitled to when you enter a hospital. Verify with your local attorney or state bar association (see index for listing) any changes in the language. However, since these regulations are derived from the federal law (PSDA), what follows is a statement of your rights.

Patient's Bill of Rights

As a patient in a hospital in New York State, you have the right, consistent with law, to:

(1) Understand and use these rights. If for any reason you do not understand or you need help, the hospital must provide assistance, including an interpreter.

(2) Receive treatment without discrimination as to race, color, religion, national origin, disability, sexual orientation, or source of payment.

(3) Receive considerate and respectful care in a clean and safe environment free of unnecessary restraints.

(4) Receive emergency care if you need it.

(5) Be informed of the name and position of the doctor who will be in charge of your care in the hospital.

(6) Know the names, positions, and functions of any hospital staff involved in your care and refuse their treatment, examination, or observation.

(7) A no smoking room.

(8) Receive complete information about your diagnosis, treatment, and prognosis.

(9) Receive all the information that you need to give informed consent for any proposed procedure or treatment. This information shall include the possible risks and benefits of the procedure or treatment.

(10) Refuse treatment and be told what effect this may have on your health.

(11) Refuse to take part in research. In deciding whether or not to participate, you have the right to a full explanation.

(12) Privacy while in the hospital and confidentiality of all information regarding your care.

(13) Participate in all decisions about your treatment and discharge from the hospital. The hospital must provide you with a written discharge plan and written description of how you can appeal your discharge.

(14) Review your medical record without charge and obtain a copy of your medical record for which the hospital can charge a reasonable fee. You cannot be denied a copy solely because you cannot afford to pay.

(15) Receive an itemized bill and explanation of all charges.

(16) Complain without fear of reprisals about the care and services you are receiving and to have the hospital respond to you, and if you request it, to have a written response. If you are not satisfied with the hospital's response, you can complain to the New York State Health Department. The hospital must provide you with the health department's telephone number.

CHAPTER 6

Do Not Resuscitate (DNR)

Repeated reference has been made to DNR orders. This, in most cases, is not an advance directive made by the patient before entering the hospital. It is rather a directive ordered by the attending physician, after consultation with and consent by the appropriate party, when the necessity for making such a decision becomes apparent.

Obviously, such a grave decision must be carefully considered and the procedure must be regulated and documented. All hospitals have a set procedure that they follow before a DNR order is issued. There is a twofold purpose for this—(1) to comply with the state laws and (2) to be scrupulously careful to avoid the possibility of being liable for damages in a lawsuit for wrongful death.

What follows is the step-by-step procedure taken by one of the major New York state hospitals prior to the issuance of a DNR order. This information is not usually made available to the public, but obviously it is important that we all be acquainted with the rigid restrictions that hospitals place upon themselves, so that we, too, can be guided in following our own course of conduct. As with everything else, state laws may vary as to what is required, but the listed intrahospital directives, requiring documentation sheets and consent forms, are essentially the same.

However, let us first understand the references that are made in the DNR regulations. The following definitions apply:

A. ADULT. Any person who is eighteen years of age or older, is the parent of a child, or has married. (Married individuals, despite being under the age of eighteen years, or the specified age in your state, are what the law considers emancipated, meaning that although they may be less than the age of adulthood, they are free to make their own decisions by reason of their married state and do not legally require the consent of parent or guardian.)

B. ATTENDING PHYSICIAN. The physician selected by or assigned to a patient who has primary responsibility for the treatment and care of the patient. More than one physician sharing the responsibility may be the attending physician.

C. CAPACITY. The ability to understand and appreciate the nature and consequences of a DNR order and to reach an informed decision regarding a DNR order. *Every adult patient is presumed to have capacity.*

D. **CARDIOPULMONARY RESUSCITATION (CPR).** Measures to restore and revive heart functions and/or to support ventilation (breathing) in the event of a heart attack.

E. **CLOSE FRIEND.** Any person eighteen years or older presenting an affidavit to an attending physician stating that he or she is a close friend and is familiar with the patient's activities, health, or religious or moral beliefs.

F. **CONCURRING PHYSICIAN.** A physician (other than the attending physician) selected to provide a concurring (agreeing) opinion. The concurring physician must have similar credentials.

G. **DEVELOPMENTAL DISABILITY.** A disability of a patient caused by mental retardation, cerebral palsy, or other neurological impairment that had begun before the patient reached the age of eighteen years. The disability must be expected to continue indefinitely and must constitute a hardship to the patient's ability to function in a normal society.

H. **DISPUTE MEDIATION SYSTEM.** A committee designated by the hospital to mediate any dispute with reference to the sufficiency of the consent of the DNR order. This mediation is not limited to disputes between a patient and his or her attending physician but will include disputes with other members of the family who are consulted and any other surrogate who is authorized to give consent.

I. **EMERGENCY MEDICAL SERVICES PERSONNEL.** The personnel of a hospital engaged in providing initial emergency services. Examples are: first responders, emergency-services attending physicians, and all other physicians and nurses assigned to the hospital's emergency service.

J. **MEDICALLY FUTILE.** CPR will be unsuccessful in restoring cardiac or respiratory function or the patient will experience repeated arrests in a short period of time before death occurs.

K. **MENTAL ILLNESS.** An affliction with a mental disease that is accompanied by a disorder or disturbance in behavior, feeling, thinking, or judgment to such an extent that the patient requires care, treatment, and rehabilitation for that disease or condition. (Alzheimer's disease is not mental illness.)

L. **PREVIOUSLY CONSENTED.** Consent to a future DNR order by a patient while still competent to give that consent. It must be given (1) in writing, signed and dated by the patient in the presence of two witnesses who also sign the document, or (2) while the patient is an inpatient in the hospital, orally in the presence of two witnesses, one of whom is a physician affiliated with the hospital, and recorded in the patient's medical record.

M. **SURROGATE.** A person selected to make decisions regarding a DNR order on behalf of a patient. The surrogate must be selected from the accompanying list in the order of priority listed. (In the event an individual is not reasonably available, or willing, or competent to make a decision regarding a DNR order, the surrogate should be selected from among the individuals in the next category.)

1. A court-appointed committee or guardian
2. The spouse
3. A son or a daughter, aged eighteen or older
4. A parent
5. A brother or sister, aged eighteen or older
6. A close friend

N. CONSENT TO **CPR** AND **DNR** ORDERS. Every patient admitted to the hospital is presumed to have consented to CPR unless a DNR order is written in the patient's chart according to the requirements set forth here. This means that unless there is a specific request for DNR, the hospital will automatically proceed with the CPR treatment.

O. TERMINAL CONDITION. An illness or injury from which there is no recovery and which can reasonably be expected to cause death within one year.

P. WITNESS. Any individual eighteen or older.

Q. ADULT PATIENT WITH CAPACITY. The consent of an adult patient with capacity (ability to understand what a DNR order is, to understand its consequences, and to make the decision).

R. ADULT PATIENT, THERAPEUTIC EXCEPTION. If the attending physician determines that the mere discussion of DNR would cause shock to the patient resulting in immediate and severe injury, the attending physician may issue a DNR order without first obtaining the patient's consent. However, this may be done only after:

1. Consulting with and obtaining a written concurrence from a concurring physician.
2. Ascertaining the wishes of the patient to the extent possible without subjecting the patient to the risk of immediate and severe injury.
3. Recording the reasons for not consulting the patient in the patient's chart.
4. Obtaining the consent of a health care agent who is available and would be authorized to make a decision regarding CPR, or, if there is no such agent, a surrogate (see M), unless the patient had previously consented to a DNR order.

Having defined some of the terms, let us examine the procedure, under the various scenarios. Let us assume that the patient has previously consented to a DNR order, but now lacks capacity to give consent. Under those circumstances, the physician may issue a DNR order, but he or she must certify that the condition that the patient had at the time of giving the original consent still exists.

Now, let's assume that the patient never gave consent for the order and the physician and the concurring physician agree that the patient lacks capacity. A validly designated health care agent, named in a health care proxy, with authority to do so, may consent to a DNR order on behalf of the patient. The health care agent will have all the rights of the patient with capacity, and his or her decision will be considered the same.

A third scenario involves the adult patient without capacity, without a health care agent, but with a surrogate.

A surrogate may consent to a DNR order only after the attending physician and the concurring physician determine to a reasonable degree of medical certainty that:

1. The patient has a terminal condition, or
2. The patient is permanently unconscious, or
3. The resuscitation would be medically futile, or
4. Resuscitation would impose an extraordinary burden on the patient in light of the patient's medical condition and the expected outcome of resuscitation.

A surrogate may consent orally to two persons over the age of eighteen, one of whom is a physician affiliated with the hospital, who shall record the decision in the patient's medical chart. The surrogate must make the decision based on the patient's wishes and in consideration of the patient's moral and religious beliefs, or, *if the patient's wishes are unknown, and cannot be ascertained, on the basis of the patient's best interests.* (This latter provision in effect gives the surrogate unlimited discretion. Naturally his or her decision must be based on the information supplied by the physicians, but in the last analysis, the decision is his or hers alone).

Finally, there is the situation where the adult patient is without capacity, without a health care agent, and without a surrogate. This is the most difficult scenario for the hospital. The regulations require the hospital staff to consult the legal department should this set of facts occur, because here the physician alone makes the decision. If he or she decides, after consultation with the concurring physician, that CPR would not serve any purpose and would, in fact, be medically futile, the attending physician may then issue a DNR order.

Minors

The consent of a parent who has custody, or a legal guardian, must be obtained prior to the issuance of a DNR order for a minor. When the attending physician has reason to believe that there is another parent or a noncustodial parent who has not been informed of a decision to issue a DNR order, that physician must make a reasonable effort to determine if the parent or noncustodial parent was in substantial and continuous contact with the minor. If so, further reasonable efforts would have to be made to notify the parent or noncustodial parent of the decision before issuing the DNR order. (Unfortunately, there are situations where neither of the parents, or designated guardian, are available for such notification. When that occurs, the hospital would have no other alternative but to have the court designate a special guardian for the specific purpose of making the DNR decision.)

The consent of a minor must also be obtained when

the attending physician, in consultation with the parent or legal guardian, determines that the minor has capacity to make the decision. Before a DNR order can be issued for a minor, the attending and concurring physician must determine with a reasonable degree of medical certainty that:

1. The patient has a terminal condition, or
2. The patient is permanently unconscious, or
3. Resuscitation would be medically futile, or
4. Resuscitation would impose an extraordinary burden on the patient in light of the patient's medical condition and the expected outcome of resuscitation. (The burden that is referred to here is the causing of the minor to remain alive.)

A custodial parent or legal guardian may consent orally to a DNR. It must be made to two persons over the age of eighteen, one of whom must be a physician affiliated with the hospital who shall record the decision in the patient's medical chart.

(Obviously, there are more stringent regulations when a minor is involved. According to the law, the minor is a ward of the court and naturally comes within the court's protection. The hospitals are aware of this and take these special measures.)

Review of DNR Orders

The attending physician must review the DNR order in light of the patient's condition. This includes review of outpatients whose DNR order is in effect while the patient is receiving care in the hospital. The review must be entered in the patient's medical record. This must be done every seven days, or sooner, if there is an improvement in the patient's condition.

Sometimes medical miracles do happen. Suppose that the patient's condition has improved so remarkably that the physician now determines that the DNR would not be appropriate. In such cases, the physician must:

1. Notify the individual who originally consented to the DNR order, and
2. Request a revocation of the DNR order.

If the revocation of the DNR order is consented to, the physician will proceed with the life-sustaining treatment. But if the person who originally gave consent to the DNR order does not now consent to its revocation, then the following steps must be taken:

1. The attending physician must transfer the case to another physician for her or his opinion, or
2. Submit the matter to the dispute mediation system.

There are instances where the DNR order has been written for a patient who at the time the DNR order was issued lacked capacity (was mentally unable to understand what was occurring) and then regains capacity to make the decision. Under those circumstances the attending physician must revoke the DNR order, apprise the patient of his or her choices, and issue another one if that is the desire of the patient. All of this must, of course, be noted in his or her medical chart. Likewise, if the patient no longer has a condition that requires a DNR order, the physician must cancel it and notify the person, other than the patient, who consented to it, as well as notifying the hospital staff responsible for the patient's care.

A mentally capable patient, or health care agent may revoke his or her consent at any time by an oral or written declaration made to a physician or member of the nursing staff.

The consent to the issuance of a DNR order does not mean a consent to the withholding of medical treatment other than CPR. (This regulation allows the administration of other treatment to make the patient comfortable, such as drug therapy for pain.)

Dispute Mediation System

In recent years, the hospitals have used the mediation board or committee for the purpose of avoiding costly law suits that are both expensive and time consuming. It benefits both sides, especially when time is of the essence.

Mediation has been put in greater use now because of the emergence of all the controversies surrounding living wills, health care proxies, and oral declarations by the patient to cease life-sustaining treatment.

While this serves a good purpose, it must be made clear that the patient, guardian, health care agent, or surrogate may still pursue his or her court remedies. In other words, it is not "compulsory arbitration," where the decision cannot be tested in court. The court will issue a ruling if the patient or someone on his or her behalf is not satisfied with the decision.

Usually, in most hospitals, there is a person in charge of professional affairs who provides information about the mediation system in the institution and how to proceed. Once a matter has been submitted to the mediation committee or board, the DNR order will be temporarily revoked, but a decision must be made within seventy-two hours. In the event that the seventy-two hours have passed and the dispute refers to the request of the patient (or his or her representative) for a DNR order, and the physician in charge has refused to issue the order, the matter must be transferred to another physician. (The regulations are silent as to what happens if the second physician, like the first, refuses to issue the order. It would appear that the only course would then be a court action. Likewise, it would also appear, although the regulations are silent, that the hospital physician *will* conform with the request if the mediation committee finds in favor of the patient.)

If the patient is transferred to the hospital from a facility licensed by the office of mental health or the office of mental disabilities (check the name that the institutions are given in your state), notice of any DNR order must be given to the director of such institution. The director has the right to object to the issuance of a DNR order. If he or she does, the matter must be referred to dispute mediation.

If the patient is transferred from another hospital,

and a DNR order had been written for him or her in the first hospital, *the DNR order will remain in effect until the attending physician first examines the transferred patient,* and either:

1. Issues an order continuing the DNR order. This can be done without notice to or consent by anyone, or
2. Cancels the DNR order provided the attending physician immediately notifies the person who consented to the order and the hospital staff directly responsible for the patient's care. (This action by the physician can, of course, be directly appealed to the mediation service.)

Information to be Supplied to Patients

Since the passage of the Patient Self Determination Act, all of the states have passed some legislation or regulations that require medical facilities to give patients and/ or residents (and where the patients or residents lack capacity, families or other adults who speak for them) copies of these laws and regulations concerning their rights as patients. These include, of course, their rights to refuse life-sustaining treatment.

Pursuant to the act, this information must be made known to the patients or their representatives. Your state's health department has literature that should be very informative. In some states, the hospitals are required to furnish the literature. In New York, for example, a document prepared by the State Department of

Health entitled "Planning in Advance for Your Medical Treatment" must be supplied to patients. They must also be furnished with the department's pamphlet entitled "Appointing Your Health Care Agent—The New York State's Proxy Law," and finally, they must be supplied with the facility's policy that summarizes the implementation of these rights.

As stated, the various states may vary as to how this information will be dispensed to the patient, either through written notices, pamphlets, or perhaps even orally, but the law is clear. *The information must be made known to the patient, or if he or she is not capable, to the person acting for him or her, at or prior to admission.*

Many states require that both inpatients *and* outpatients be informed. However, outpatients need receive the information only one time, and not each time that they seek care as outpatients at a particular institution.

Most hospitals will, for their own protection, assess any advance directives, such as living wills and health care proxies, to be sure that they comply with local law and that the language expresses the "clear and convincing" intent that is required when a patient requests that life-sustaining treatment be withheld or withdrawn. The facility may, but is not required to, seek a court determination as to whether an advance directive has been expressed in a clear and convincing manner.

Finally, the regulations require nursing homes to educate residents concerning health care proxies. The purpose of this is to ensure that each resident who creates a proxy while residing in the facility does so voluntarily. Many states, including New York, require that the homes designate one or more individuals who will respond to questions and assist residents with respect to proxies in general.

In conclusion, it is obvious that you have an absolute right to be completely informed about your options in making decisions about your medical care. This specifically includes your right to refuse medical or surgical treatment. The Patient Self Determination Act specifies that the facility must supply you with written information *about the policies of the institution in carrying out the provisions of the law.* And it is important to note that it is a violation of the act for any institution to discriminate against an individual based on whether or not he or she has executed an advance directive. Likewise, it is a violation to keep you uneducated about your choices after you enter the facility. If you enter as a patient, or are the representative of the patient, ask for a copy of the hospital's policy regarding the implementation of the rights guaranteed under the act. It *must* be given to you.

In the following pages you will find the various forms I have referred to in this chapter. They are, in order of appearance:

A. Order Not To Resuscitate (DNR Order)
B. Consent To DNR Order by Health Care Agent
C. Consent To DNR Order by Surrogate
D. Consent To DNR Order by Parent/Legal Guardian
E. Affidavit Of Close Friend
F. Consent To DNR Order by Adult Patient With Capacity

You will also find intrahospital forms—documents that are not normally made known or available to the public. They indicate the precise steps that must be taken when DNR orders are to be issued in all of the following circumstances:

1. Adult patient with capacity
2. Adult patient, therapeutic exception (where discussion of CPR would cause immediate and severe injury)
3. Adult patient without capacity who previously consented to a DNR order
4. Adult patient without capacity and with a health care agent
5. Adult patient without capacity and without a health care agent who has a surrogate
6. Adult patient without capacity and who has no health care agent or surrogate
7. Minor patient

You can see by reading these documents that the steps taken are precisely detailed. It gives the reader a wider understanding of his or her rights when these details are made known. These are the regulations promulgated by one hospital for the purpose of conforming with the Patient Self Determination Act. All medical facilities must conform. While the manner in which they do varies, and the specific procedures that one hospital has set for itself may not be the same as another, the objectives are the same.

ORDER NOT TO RESUSCITATE
(DNR ORDER)

Person's Name_____

Date of Birth_____ /_____ /_____

<u>Do not resuscitate the person named above</u>

   Physician's Signature_____

   Print Name_____

   License Number_____

   Date_____ /_____ /_____

It is the responsibility of the physician to determine, at least every 90 days, whether this order continues to be appropriate, and to indicate this by a note in the person's medical chart. The issuance of a new form is NOT required, and under the law this order shall be considered valid unless it is known that it has been revoked. This order remains valid and must be followed, even if it has not been reviewed within the 90 day period.

CONSENT TO DNR ORDER
BY HEALTH CARE AGENT

1. I hereby authorize Dr._____to issue a DNR order on the patient_____. I understand this means that cardiopulmonary resuscitation will be withheld in the event his/her heart stops beating or he/she stops breathing.

2. Dr._____has explained to me the patient's diagnosis and prognosis, and the range of available measures, the reasonably foreseeable risks and benefits of cardiopulmonary resuscitation, and the consequences of an order not to resuscitate the patient.

3. I am making this decision based on my authority as the patient's Health Care Agent.

4. I confirm that I have read and fully understand the above and that all blank spaces have been completed prior to my signing.

CONSENT BY HEALTH CARE AGENT

_____   _____
Signature   Print Name

_____
Date

WITNESS CERTIFICATION

_____   _____
Signature   Print Name

_____   _____
Title/Relationship to Patient   Date

CONSENT TO DNR ORDER
BY SURROGATE

1. I hereby authorize Dr._____to issue a DNR order on the patient_____. I understand this means that cardiopulmonary resuscitation will be withheld in the event his/her heart stops beating or he/she stops breathing.

2. Dr._____has explained to me the patient's diagnosis and prognosis, the range of available resuscitation measures, the reasonable foreseeable risks and benefits of cardiopulmonary resuscitation, and the consequences of an order not to resuscitate the patient.

3. I am making this decision based on (circle one)
   a. the patient's own wishes
   b. the patient's best interests, since the patient's wishes are unknown and can not be ascertained.

4. My relationship to the patient is as follows (circle one)
   a. the court appointed committee or guardian of patient
   b. the spouse
   c. a son or daughter, aged 18 or older
   d. a parent
   e. a brother or sister, aged 18 or older

   _____   _____
   Name of Surrogate   Relationship of Surrogate

5. To the best of my knowledge there is no one higher on the list in Section 4 above available to consent on behalf of the patient.

6. I confirm that I have read and fully understand the above and that all blank spaces have been completed prior to my signing.

CONSENT BY SURROGATE

_____   _____
Signature   Print Name

_____
Date

(continued)

WITNESS CERTIFICATION

_____   _____
Signature   Print Name

_____   _____
Title/Relationship to Patient   Date

CONSENT TO DNR ORDER
BY PARENT/LEGAL GUARDIAN

1. I hereby authorize Dr._____to issue a DNR order for my child_____. I understand this means that cardiopulmonary resuscitation will be withheld in the event that his/her heart stops beating or he/she stops breathing.

2. Dr._____has explained to me my child's diagnosis and prognosis, the range of available resuscitation measures, the reasonable foreseeable risks and benefits of cardiopulmonary resuscitation, and the consequences of an order not to resuscitate my child. In making this decision, I have considered my child's wishes to the extent they can be known to me including his/her religious beliefs.

3. I confirm that I have read and fully understand the above and that all blank spaces have been completed prior to my signing.

_____   _____
Signature of Parent/Legal   Print name
Guardian

_____   _____
Relationship to Patient   Date

WITNESS CERTIFICATION

_____   _____
Signature   Print Name

_____   _____
Title/Relationship to Patient   Date

AFFIDAVIT OF CLOSE FRIEND

_____ being duly sworn, deposes and says:
Name of Friend

1. I reside at

_____

_____

2. I am a close friend of the patient_____and have maintained such regular contact with the patient as to be familiar
with his/her activities, health, and religious or moral beliefs.

3. I base my statement that I am a close friend on the following
facts and circumstances (describe relationship with patient, fre-
quency of contacts, etc.):

_____

_____

_____

_____
Signature

Sworn to before me this_____day of_____1993

_____
Notary Public

CONSENT TO DNR ORDER
BY ADULT PATIENT WITH CAPACITY

1. I hereby authorize Dr._____to issue a DNR order on myself, _____. I understand this means that cardiopulmonary resuscitation will be withheld in the event that my heart stops beating or I stop breathing.

2. Dr._____has explained to me my diagnosis and prognosis, the range of available resuscitation measures, the reasonable foreseeable risks and benefits of cardiopulmonary resuscitation, and the consequences of an order not to resuscitate me.

3. I confirm that I have read and fully understand the above and that all blank spaces have been completed prior to my signing.

_____   _____
Signature of Patient   Print Name

_____
Date

WITNESS CERTIFICATION

_____   _____
Signature   Print Name

_____   _____
Title/Relationship to Patient   Date

DNR DOCUMENTATION SHEET #1
ADULT PATIENT WITH CAPACITY

Directions: This Documentation Sheet sets forth in consecutive order the steps that must be followed before writing a DNR Order for an ADULT PATIENT WITH CAPACITY. Refer to the Hospital Center's Do Not Resuscitate Order Policy for specific definitions and applications of policy. When completed, this Sheet must be placed in the patient's medical record.

Step One—Provision of Information
The attending physician must provide the patient with information regarding CPR and a DNR Order.

ATTENDING PHYSICIAN'S STATEMENT

I have provided to the patient information about his/her diagnosis and prognosis, the range of available resuscitation measures, the reasonably foreseeable risks and benefits of cardiopulmonary resuscitation for him/her, and the consequences of a DNR Order.

_____
Signature of Attending Physician   Date

Step Two—Consent by Patient
The patient must give oral or written consent to a DNR Order at or about the time the DNR Order is to be written. Oral consent must be given during hospitalization in the presence of two witnesses, one of whom must be a physician on the staff at the Hospital Center.

WITNESS'S STATEMENT

The patient has expressed orally in my presence the decision to consent to a DNR Order, subject to the following conditions or limitations (if any):

(continued)

_____

_____

_____

Signature of Witness	Printed Name of Witness Date

_____

Title/Relationship to Patient	Date

_____

Signature of Physician Witness	Printed Name of Date Physician Witness

Instead of oral consent, the patient may choose to consent to the DNR Order in writing. Written consent must be signed by the patient and two witnesses. A copy of the written consent must be placed in the medical record.

Step Three—Actions Taken by Attending Physician
The attending physician must promptly do one of the following and note the action taken:

_____ a. issue the DNR Order, or issue the order at such time as any conditions specified in the patient's decision are met; or

_____ b. make his/her objections to the DNR Order and the reasons known to the patient and either transfer the patient to another attending physician; or

_____ c. refer the matter to the Dispute Mediation System.

The DNR Order must be reviewed every seven days, or sooner if there is an improvement in the patient's condition. This review must be documented in the patient's medical record.

DNR DOCUMENTATION SHEET #2
ADULT PATIENT
THERAPEUTIC EXCEPTION

Directions: This Documentation Sheet sets forth in consecutive order the steps that must be followed before writing a DNR Order for an **ADULT PATIENT WHO WOULD SUFFER AN IMMEDIATE AND SEVERE INJURY FROM A DISCUSSION OF CPR.** Refer to the Hospital Center's Do Not Resuscitate Order Policy for specific definitions and applications of policy. When completed, this Sheet must be placed in the patient's medical record.

Step One—Attending Physician's Determination of Injury
The attending physician must determine that the patient would suffer immediate and severe injury from a discussion of CPR, and must then ascertain the wishes of the patient to the extent possible without subjecting the patient to risk.

ATTENDING PHYSICIAN'S STATEMENT

I have determined to a reasonable degree of medical certainty that the patient would suffer immediate and severe injury from a discussion of CPR because

_____

_____

I have ascertained the wishes of the patient to the extent possible without subjecting the patient to risk.

_____
Signature of Attending Physician   Date

Step Two—Concurring Physician's Determination of Injury
A concurring physician must agree with the determination that the patient would suffer immediate and severe injury from a discussion of CPR.

(continued)

CONCURRING PHYSICIAN'S STATEMENT

I have personally examined the patient and have determined to a reasonable degree of medical certainty that the patient would suffer immediate and severe injury from a discussion of CPR.

_____
Signature of Concurring Physician   Date

Step Three—Previous Consent
The attending physician must determine whether the patient previously consented to a DNR Order. If the patient previously consented, documentation of that consent must be attached to this Documentation Sheet. The attending physician must review the previous consent and determine that any specified medical conditions described in that document exist.

ATTENDING PHYSICIAN'S STATEMENT

I have personally examined the patient and have determined to a reasonable degree of medical certainty that the medical conditions described in the patient's previous consent to a DNR Order exist.

_____
Signature of Attending Physician   Date

Step Four—Determination of Suitability for DNR Order
(If the patient previously consented, proceed to Step Seven)

If the patient has not previously consented to a DNR Order, the attending physician must determine that the patient is suitable for the issuance of a DNR Order. A concurring physician must agree with this determination.

(continued)

ATTENDING AND CONCURRING PHYSICIANS' STATEMENT

I have personally examined the patient and have determined to a reasonable degree of medical certainty that: (check as applicable):

_____ a. the patient has a terminal condition; or

_____ b. resuscitation would be medically futile; or

_____ c. resuscitation would impose an extraordinary burden on the patient in light of the patient's medical condition and the expected outcome of resuscitation for the patient.

_____
Signature of Attending Physician   Date

_____
Signature of Concurring Physician   Date

Step Five—Identification of Health Care Agent or Surrogate

If there is no evidence that the patient previously consented to a DNR Order, the attending physician must determine who is the proper health care agent or, if there is none, the surrogate. The surrogate must be selected from the following list, in order of priority listed.

a. the court-appointed committee or guardian of the patient

b. the spouse

c. a son or daughter, aged 18 or older

d. a parent

e. a brother or sister, aged 18 or older

f. a close friend

_____   _____
Name of Health Care Agent   Relationship of Surrogate
or Surrogate   to Patient

(continued)

Step Six—Provision of Information to and Consent From Health Care Agent or Surrogate

The attending physician must provide the health care agent or, if there is none, the surrogate, with information regarding CPR and a DNR Order. The health care agent or, if there is none, the surrogate, must give oral or written consent to a DNR Order at or about the time the DNR Order is to be written. Written consent must be documented on, depending on who gives consent, either the "Consent By Health Care Agent To DNR Order" or "Consent By Surrogate To DNR Order" form, a copy of which is attached. Oral consent must be given in the presence of two witnesses, one of whom must be a physician on the staff at the Hospital Center, and recorded in the patient's medical record.

WITNESS'S STATEMENT

The health care agent or surrogate has expressed orally in my presence the decision to consent to a DNR Order, subject to the following conditions or limitations (if any):

_____

_____

_____	_____
Signature of Witness	Printed Name of Witness Date
_____	_____
Title/Relationship to Patient	Date
_____	_____
Signature of Physician Witness	Printed Name of Date Physician Witness

Instead of oral consent, the health care agent may choose to consent to the DNR Order in writing. Written consent must be documented on the form entitled "Consent by Health Care Agent to DNR Order", a copy of which is attached to this Documentation Sheet. A witness must sign this form.

(continued)

The attending physician must obtain the consent of the health care agent or, if there is none, the surrogate, which must be documented on the "Consent By Health Care Agent Or Surrogate To DNR Order" form attached to this Documentation Sheet. A witness must sign this form.

Step Seven—Actions Taken by Attending Physician
The attending physician must promptly do one of the following and note the action taken:

____ a. issue the DNR Order; or

____ b. if he/she has actual notice that the health care agent or someone on the surrogates list objects to the DNR Order, refer the matter to the Dispute Mediation System; or

____ c. object to issuing the DNR Order and either transfer the patient to another attending physician or refer the matter to the Dispute Mediation System.

The DNR Order must be reviewed every seven days, or sooner if there is an improvement in the patient's condition. This review must be documented in the patient's medical record. The patient's risk of injury from a discussion of CPR must also be reassessed by the attending physician on a regular basis.

DNR DOCUMENTATION SHEET #3
ADULT PATIENT WITHOUT CAPACITY
WHO PREVIOUSLY CONSENTED TO A DNR ORDER

Directions: This Documentation Sheet sets forth in consecutive order the steps that must be followed before writing a DNR Order for an ADULT PATIENT WITHOUT CAPACITY WHO PREVIOUSLY CONSENTED TO A DNR ORDER. Refer to the Hospital Center's Do Not Resuscitate Order Policy for specific definitions and applications of policy. When completed, this Sheet must be placed in the patient's medical record.

Step One—Attending Physician's Determination of Incapacity
The attending physician must determine that the patient lacks capacity.

DETERMINATION OF INCAPACITY

I have examined the patient and have determined to a reasonable degree of medical certainty that he/she lacks the ability to understand and appreciate the nature and consequences of a DNR Order, including the benefits and disadvantages, and to reach an informed decision. In my opinion, the cause and nature of the patient's incapacity are:

_____

_____

and its extent and probable duration are:

_____

_____
Signature of Attending Physician   Date

Step Two—Concurring Physician's Determination of Incapacity
The determination of incapacity must also be determined and agreed to by a concurring physician. If the patient's incapacity is

(continued)

due to a developmental disability or mental illness, the concurring opinion must be provided by a physician with specialized training.

CONCURRING PHYSICIAN'S STATEMENT

I have personally examined the patient and have determined to a reasonable degree of medical certainty that he/she lacks the ability to understand and appreciate the nature and consequences of a DNR Order, including the benefits and disadvantages, and to reach an informed decision. In my opinion, the cause and nature of the incapacity are:

_____

_____

and its extent and probable duration are:

_____

_____
Signature of Concurring Physician   Date

Step Three—Identification of Health Care Agent or Surrogate
The attending physician must determine who is the proper health care agent or, if there is none, the surrogate. The surrogate must be selected from the following list, in order of priority listed.

a. the court-appointed committee or guardian of the patient

b. the spouse

c. a son or daughter, aged 18 or older

d. a parent

e. a brother or sister, aged 18 or older

f. a close friend

_____   _____
Name of Health Care Agent   Relationship of Surrogate
or Surrogate   to Patient

(continued)

Step Four—Notice to Patient, Health Care Agent, or Surrogate
The attending physician must notify the health care agent or surrogate of the determination that the patient lacks capacity. In addition, if there is any indication of the patient's ability to understand, notice must be given to the patient, together with a copy of the Department of Health's DNR Statement of Rights.

NOTICE TO PATIENT, HEALTH CARE AGENT, OR SURROGATE OF LACK OF CAPACITY

I have provided notice of the determination of the patient's lack of capacity to the health care agent or, if there is none, to the surrogate; and (check one)

____ a. there is no indication of the patient's ability to comprehend such notice and I am therefore not providing notice to the patient; or

____ b. I have given the patient notice of the determination.

Signature of Attending Physician   Date

Step Five—Documentation of Previous Consent
The attending physician must obtain documentation that the patient previously consented to a DNR Order and attach such documentation to this Documentation Sheet. The attending physician must review the previous consent and determine that any specific medical conditions described in that document exist.

DETERMINATION OF MEDICAL CONDITIONS

I have personally examined the patient and have determined to a reasonable degree of medical certainty that the medical conditions described in the patient's previous consent to a DNR Order exist.

Signature of Attending Physician   Date

(continued)

Step Six—Actions Taken by Attending Physician
The attending physician must promptly do one of the following
and note the action taken:

___a. issue the DNR Order, or issue the order at such time as
any conditions specified in the patient's decision are
met; or

___b. if she/he has actual notice that the health care agent or
the surrogate objects to the DNR Order, refer the matter
to the Dispute Mediation System; or

___c. object to the issuance of the DNR Order and either
transfer the patient to another attending physician or
refer the matter to the Dispute Mediation System.

The DNR Order must be reviewed every seven days, or sooner if
there is an improvement in the patient's condition. This review
must be documented in the patient's medical record.

DNR DOCUMENTATION SHEET #4
ADULT PATIENT WITHOUT CAPACITY
AND WITH A HEALTH CARE AGENT

Directions: This Documentation Sheet sets forth in consecutive order the steps that must be followed before writing a DNR Order for an ADULT PATIENT WITHOUT CAPACITY WHO HAS A HEALTH CARE AGENT. Refer to the Hospital Center's Do Not Resuscitate Order Policy for specific definitions and applications of policy. When completed, this Sheet must be placed in the patient's medical record.

Step One—Attending Physician's Determination of Incapacity
The attending physician must determine that the patient lacks capacity.

ATTENDING PHYSICIAN'S STATEMENT

I have examined the patient and have determined to a reasonable degree of medical certainty that he/she lacks the ability to understand and appreciate the nature and consequences of a DNR Order, including the benefits and disadvantages, and to reach an informed decision. In my opinion, the cause and nature of the patient's incapacity are:

_____

_____

and its extent and probable duration are:

_____

_____

Signature of Attending Physician   Date

Step Two—Concurring Physician's Determination of Incapacity
The determination of incapacity must also be determined and agreed to by a concurring physician. If the patient's incapacity

(continued)

is due to a developmental disability or mental illness, the concurring opinion must be provided by a physician with specialized training.

CONCURRING PHYSICIAN'S STATEMENT

I have personally examined the patient and have determined to a reasonable degree of medical certainty that he/she lacks the ability to understand and appreciate the nature and consequences of a DNR Order, including the benefits and disadvantages, and to reach an informed decision. In my opinion, the cause and nature of the incapacity are:

_____

_____

and its extent and probable duration are:

_____

_____

Signature of Concurring Physician   Date

Step Three—Notice to Health Care Agent of Incapacity
The attending physician must notify the health care agent of the determination that the patient lacks capacity. In addition, if there is any indication of the patient's ability to understand, notice must be given to the patient, together with a copy of the Department of Health's DNR Statement of Rights.

NOTICE TO PATIENT AND HEALTH CARE AGENT OF LACK OF CAPACITY

I have provided notice of the determination of the patient's lack of capacity to the health care agent and (check one)

_____a. there is no indication of the patient's ability to comprehend such notice and I am therefore not providing notice to the patient; or

(continued)

___ b. I have given the patient notice of the determination.

_____

Signature of Attending Physician   Date

Step Four—Provision of Information to and Consent from Health Care Agent

The attending physician must provide the health care agent with information regarding CPR and a DNR Order. The health care agent must give oral or written consent to a DNR Order at or about the time the DNR Order is to be written. Oral consent must be given in the presence of two witnesses, one of whom must be a physician on the staff at the Hospital Center, and recorded in the patient's medical record.

WITNESS'S STATEMENT

The health care agent has expressed orally in my presence the decision to consent to a DNR Order, subject to the following conditions or limitations (if any):

_____

_____

_____   _____
Signature of Witness   Printed Name of Witness   Date

_____   _____
Title/Relationship to Patient   Date

_____   _____
Signature of Physician Witness   Printed Name of   Date
                                 Physician Witness

Instead of oral consent, the health care agent may choose to consent to the DNR Order in writing. Written consent must be documented on the form entitled "Consent by Health Care Agent to DNR Order", a copy of which is attached to this Documentation Sheet. A witness must sign this form.

(continued)

Step Five—Notice to Patient of DNR Order
If there is any indication of the patient's ability to comprehend, and the attending physician has not determined that the patient would suffer immediate and severe injury from a discussion of CPR, notice of the health care agent's decision must be provided to the patient.

NOTICE OF DNR TO PATIENT

Check one:

___ a. I have determined that the patient has not given any indication of ability to comprehend, and I am not therefore providing notice of the health care agent's decision to the patient; or

___ b. I have determined that the patient would suffer immediate and severe injury from a discussion of CPR, and I am not therefore providing notice of the health care agent's decision to the patient; or

___ c. Neither a. or b. apply and I have provided notice of the health care agent's decision to the patient.

_____
Signature of Attending Physician   Date

NOTE: IF THE PATIENT OBJECTS, A DNR ORDER MUST NOT BE ISSUED.

Step Six—Actions Taken by Attending Physician
The attending physician must promptly do one of the following and note the action taken:

___ a. issue the DNR Order, or issue the order at such time as any conditions specified in the health care agent's decision are met; or

(continued)

____ b. make his/her objections to the DNR Order and the reasons known to the health care agent and either transfer
the patient to another attending physician; or

____ c. refer the matter to the Dispute Mediation System.

The DNR Order must be reviewed every seven days, or sooner if
there is an improvement in the patient's condition. This review
must be documented in the patient's medical record.

DNR DOCUMENTATION SHEET #5
ADULT PATIENT WITHOUT CAPACITY
AND WITHOUT A HEALTH CARE AGENT
WHO HAS A SURROGATE

Directions: This Documentation Sheet sets forth in consecutive order the steps that must be followed before writing a DNR Order for an ADULT PATIENT WITHOUT CAPACITY AND WITHOUT A HEALTH CARE AGENT WHO HAS A SURROGATE. Refer to the Hospital Center's Do Not Resuscitate Order Policy for specific definitions and applications of policy. When completed, this Sheet must be placed in the patient's medical record.

Step One—Attending Physician's Determination of Incapacity
The attending physician must determine that the patient lacks capacity.

DETERMINATION OF INCAPACITY

I have examined the patient and have determined to a reasonable degree of medical certainty that he/she lacks the ability to understand and appreciate the nature and consequences of a DNR Order, including the benefits and disadvantages, and to reach an informed decision. In my opinion, the cause and nature of the patient's incapacity are:

_____

_____

and its extent and probable duration are:

_____

_____
Signature of Attending Physician   Date

Step Two—Concurring Physician's Determination of Incapacity
The determination of incapacity must also be determined and
(continued)

agreed to by a concurring physician. If the patient's incapacity is due to a developmental disability or mental illness, the concurring opinion must be provided by a physician with specialized training.

CONCURRING PHYSICIAN'S STATEMENT

I have personally examined the patient and have determined to a reasonable degree of medical certainty that he/she lacks the ability to understand and appreciate the nature and consequences of a DNR Order, including the benefits and disadvantages, and to reach an informed decision. In my opinion, the cause and nature of the incapacity are:

_____

_____

and its extent and probable duration are:

_____

_____

Signature of Attending Physician   Date

Step Three—Identification of a Surrogate
The attending physician must determine who is the proper surrogate. The surrogate must be selected from the following list, in order of priority listed.

   a. the court-appointed committee or guardian of the patient

   b. the spouse

   c. a son or daughter, aged 18 or older

   d. a parent

   e. a brother or sister, aged 18 or older

   f. a close friend

_____   _____

Name of Surrogate   Relationship of Surrogate to Patient

(continued)

Step Four—Notice to Surrogate of Incapacity
The attending physician must notify the surrogate of the determination that the patient lacks capacity. In addition, if there is any indication of the patient's ability to understand, notice must be given to the patient, together with a copy of the Department of Health's DNR Statement of Rights.

NOTICE TO PATIENT AND SURROGATE OF LACK OF CAPACITY

I have provided notice of the determination of the patient's lack of capacity to the surrogate and (check one)

_____ a. there is no indication of the patient's ability to comprehend such notice and I am therefore not providing notice to the patient; or

_____ b. I have given the patient notice of the determination.

_____
Signature of Attending Physician   Date

Step Five—Determination of Suitability for DNR Order
The attending physician must determine that the patient is suitable for the issuance of a DNR Order. A concurring physician must agree with the determination.

DETERMINATION OF SUITABILITY FOR DNR ORDER

I have personally examined the patient and I have determined to a reasonable degree of medical certainty that: (check as applicable)

_____ a. the patient has a terminal condition; or

_____ b. the patient is permanently unconscious; or

_____ c. resuscitation would be medically futile; or

(continued)

___ d. resuscitation would impose an extraordinary burden on the patient in light of the patient's medical condition and the expected outcome of resuscitation for the patient.

_____
Signature of Attending Physician   Date

_____
Signature of Concurring Physician   Date

Step Six—Provision of Information to and Consent From Surrogate
The attending physician must provide the surrogate with information regarding CPR and a DNR Order.

The surrogate must give oral or written consent to the DNR Order at or about the time the DNR Order is to be written. Oral consent must be given in the presence of two witnesses, one of whom must be a physician on the staff at the Hospital Center, and recorded in the patient's medical record.

WITNESS'S STATEMENT

The surrogate has expressed orally in my presence the decision to consent to a DNR Order, subject to the following conditions or limitations (if any):

_____

_____

_____   _____
Signature of Witness   Printed Name of Witness   Date

_____   _____
Title/Relationship to Patient   Date

_____   _____
Signature of Physician Witness   Printed Name of   Date
                                   Physician Witness

(continued)

Instead of oral consent, the surrogate may choose to consent to the DNR Order in writing. Written consent must be documented on the form entitled "Consent By Surrogate To DNR Order", a copy of which is attached to this Documentation Sheet. A witness must sign this form.

Step Seven—Notice to Patient of DNR Order
If there is any indication of the patient's ability to comprehend, and the attending physician has not determined that the patient would suffer immediate and severe injury from a discussion of CPR, notice of the surrogate's decision must be provided to the patient.

NOTICE OF DNR TO PATIENT

Check one:

___ a. I have determined that the patient has not given any indication of ability to comprehend, and I am not therefore providing notice of the surrogate's decision to the patient; or

___ b. I have determined that the patient would suffer immediate and severe injury from a discussion of CPR, and I am not therefore providing notice of the surrogate's decision to the patient; or

___ c. Neither a. or b. apply and I have provided notice of the surrogate's decision to the patient.

_____
Signature of Attending Physician   Date

NOTE: IF THE PATIENT OBJECTS, A DNR ORDER MUST NOT BE ISSUED

Step Eight—Actions Taken by Attending Physician
The attending physician must promptly do one of the following and note the action taken:

(continued)

____ a. issue the DNR Order, or issue the order at such time as any conditions specified in the surrogate's decision are met; or

____ b. make his/her objections to the DNR Order and the reasons known to the surrogate and either transfer the patient to another attending physician; or

____ c. refer the matter to the Dispute Mediation System.

The DNR Order must be reviewed every seven days, or sooner if there is an improvement in the patient's condition. This review must be documented in the patient's medical record.

DNR DOCUMENTATION SHEET #6
ADULT PATIENT WITHOUT CAPACITY AND
WHO HAS NO HEALTH CARE AGENT OR SURROGATE

Directions: This Documentation Sheet sets forth in consecutive order the steps that must be followed before writing a DNR Order for an ADULT PATIENT WITHOUT CAPACITY AND WHO HAS NO HEALTH CARE AGENT OR SURROGATE. Refer to the Hospital Center's Do Not Resuscitate Order Policy for specific definitions and applications of policy. When completed, this Sheet must be placed in the patient's medical record.

Step One—Attending Physician's Determination of Incapacity
The attending physician must determine that the patient lacks capacity.

DETERMINATION OF INCAPACITY

I have examined the patient and have determined to a reasonable degree of medical certainty that he/she lacks the ability to understand and appreciate the nature and consequences of a DNR Order, including the benefits and disadvantages, and to reach an informed decision. In my opinion, the cause and nature of the patient's incapacity are:

_____

_____

and its extent and probable duration are:

_____

_____
Signature of Attending Physician   Date

Step Two—Concurring Physician's Determination of Incapacity
The determination of incapacity must also be determined and
(continued)

agreed to by a concurring physician. If the patient's incapacity is due to a developmental disability or mental illness, the concurring opinion must be provided by a physician with specialized training.

CONCURRING PHYSICIAN'S STATEMENT

I have personally examined the patient and have determined to a reasonable degree of medical certainty that he/she lacks the ability to understand and appreciate the nature and consequences of a DNR Order, including the benefits and disadvantages, and to reach an informed decision. In my opinion, the cause and nature of the incapacity are:

_____

_____

and its extent and probable duration are:

_____

_____
Signature of Concurring Physician   Date

Step Three—Determination That There is no Health Care Agent or Surrogate
The attending physician must have determined that there is no health care agent or that a surrogate is not available from the following list:

  a. the court-appointed committee or guardian of the patient

  b. the spouse

  c. a son or daughter, aged 18 or older

  d. a parent

  e. a brother or sister, aged 18 or older

  f. a close friend

(continued)

ATTENDING PHYSICIAN'S STATEMENT

I have determined that there is no health care agent or surrogate available to consent for the patient.

_____
Signature of Attending Physician   Date

Step Four—Notice to Patient of DNR Order
If there is any indication of the patient's ability to comprehend, and the attending physician has not determined that the patient would suffer immediate and severe injury from a discussion of CPR, notice of the health care agent's decision must be provided to the patient.

NOTICE OF DNR TO PATIENT

Check one:

____ a. I have determined that the patient has not given any indication of ability to comprehend, and I am not therefore providing notice of the decision to the patient; or

____ b. I have determined that the patient would suffer immediate and severe injury from a discussion of CPR, and I am not therefore providing notice of the decision to the patient; or

____ c. Neither a. or b. apply and I have provided notice of the decision to the patient.

_____
Signature of Attending Physician   Date

NOTE: IF THE PATIENT OBJECTS, A DNR ORDER MUST
NOT BE ISSUED.

Step Five—Determination of Medical Futility
The attending physician must determine that CPR would be medically futile. A concurring physician must agree with the determination.

(continued)

DETERMINATION OF MEDICAL FUTILITY

I have personally examined the patient and I have determined to a reasonable degree of medical certainty that CPR would be medically futile.

_____

Signature of Attending Physician   Date

_____

Signature of Concurring Physician   Date

If the attending physician determines that CPR would not be medically futile but that a DNR Order should nonetheless be written, the Legal Department should be consulted.

Step Six—Notice to Patient of DNR Order

If there is any indication of the patient's ability to comprehend, and the attending physician has not determined that the patient would suffer immediate and severe injury from a discussion of CPR, notice of the physician's decision must be provided to the patient.

NOTICE OF DNR TO PATIENT

Check one:

____ a. I have determined that the patient has not given any indication of ability to comprehend, and I am not therefore providing notice of the decision; or

____ b. I have determined that the patient would suffer immediate and severe injury from a discussion of CPR, and I am not therefore providing notice of the decision to the patient; or

____ c. Neither a. or b. apply and I have provided notice of the decision to the patient.

_____

Signature of Attending Physician   Date

(continued)

NOTE: IF THE PATIENT OBJECTS, A DNR ORDER MUST
NOT BE ISSUED

Step Seven—Actions Taken by Attending Physician
The attending physician may now issue the DNR Order.

The DNR Order must be reviewed every seven days, or sooner if there is an improvement in the patient's condition. This review must be documented in the patient's medical record.

DNR DOCUMENTATION SHEET #7
MINOR PATIENT

Directions: This Documentation Sheet sets forth in consecutive order the steps that must be followed before writing a DNR Order for a MINOR PATIENT. Refer to the Hospital Center's Do Not Resuscitate Order Policy for specific definitions and applications of policy. When completed, this Sheet must be placed in the patient's medical record.

Step One—Determination of Suitability
The attending physician must determine that the patient is suitable for a DNR Order. A concurring physician must agree with this determination.

ATTENDING AND CONCURRING PHYSICIANS' STATEMENT

I have personally examined the patient and have determined to a reasonable degree of medical certainty that: (check as applicable):

____ a. the patient has a terminal condition; or

____ b. the patient is permanently unconscious; or

____ c. resuscitation would be medically futile; or

____ d. resuscitation would impose an extraordinary burden on the patient in light of the patient's medical condition and the expected outcome of resuscitation for the patient.

_____
Signature of Attending Physician   Date

_____
Signature of Concurring Physician   Date

Step Two—Consent by Parent or Legal Guardian
The attending physician must obtain the consent of a parent who has custody or the legal guardian. The consent must be docu-
(continued)

mented on the "Consent By Parent/Legal Guardian To DNR Order" form attached to this Documentation Sheet. A witness must sign this form. Consent may be given orally in the presence of two witnesses, one of whom is a physician on the staff of the Hospital, and shall be recorded in the patient's medical record.

Step Three—Determination of Incapacity
The attending physician must determine, in consultation with a parent who has custody or the legal guardian, if the patient has capacity to make a decision regarding CPR.

ATTENDING PHYSICIAN'S STATEMENT

I have examined the patient and have consulted with the patient's parent/legal guardian and have determined: (check one)

____ a. the patient lacks capacity to make a decision regarding CPR; or

____ b. the patient has capacity to make a decision regarding CPR.

_____
Signature of Attending Physician   Date

Step Four—Oral Consent from Patient
If the determination has been made that the patient has capacity to make a decision, the attending physician must obtain the oral consent of the patient.

ATTENDING PHYSICIAN'S STATEMENT

The patient has expressed orally in my presence the decision to consent to a DNR Order. I have provided to the patient information about his/her diagnosis and prognosis, the range of available resuscitation measures, the reasonably foreseeable risks and benefits of CPR for him/her, and the consequences of a DNR Order.

_____
Signature of Attending Physician   Date

(continued)

WITNESS'S STATEMENT

The patient has expressed orally in my presence the decision to consent to a DNR Order.

_____   _____
Signature of Witness   Printed Name of Witness

_____   _____
Title/Relationship to Patient   Date

Step Five—Notification of Other Parent
If the attending physician has reason to believe that there is another parent, including a non-custodial parent, who has not been informed of the decision regarding a DNR Order for the patient, the attending physician must make diligent efforts to notify the other parent of this decision if it has been determined that any such parent has maintained substantial and continuous contact with the patient.

Step Six—Actions Taken by Attending Physician
The attending physician must promptly do one of the following and note the action taken: (check one)

____a. issue the DNR Order; or

____b. if he/she has actual notice that a parent or non-custodial parent objects to the DNR Order, submit the matter to the Dispute Mediation System and must not issue a DNR Order or must revoke a previously written DNR Order; or

____c. object to issuing the DNR Order, notify the parent(s)/ legal guardian of such objection, and either transfer the patient to another attending physician or refer the matter to the Dispute Mediation System.

The DNR Order must be reviewed every seven days, or sooner if there is an improvement in the patient's condition. This review must be documented in the patient's medical record.

CHAPTER 7

Viatical Settlements

Although *viatical* is a word that is not commonly used in everyday conversation, it may become known to the terminally ill. It derives from the Latin *Viaticum*—the Holy Communion given to those who are dying or in danger of imminent death.

Any discussion of living wills should include a reference to viatical settlements because they are another means of obtaining some peace of mind during a difficult time. A viatical settlement company is in the business of buying life insurance benefits from terminally ill people. The person who sells his or her benefits is called the viator. The agreement between the company and the individual is called the viatical settlement. Here is the way it works: A person agrees to assign his or her death benefits, that is, the sum that would be payable upon his or her death to the settlement company. In exchange, the company provides that individual with immediate funds, and depending on the nature of the settlement, a regular cash flow to assist in the payment of rent, medical care, and any other essential items not covered by health or disability insurance.

When properly and honestly done, this type of agreement can be a great service to the terminally ill person. His or her immediate need for additional financial resources during illness may be satisfied. Depending on the face amount of the policy, the cash proceeds may sustain the individual for the balance of his or her life. Lifestyles can be maintained with the degree of comfort and peace of mind that is achieved through financial independence.

Nevertheless, there are dangers—not in the concept of viatical settlements but in some individuals who offer such settlements. It is difficult to comprehend that some people are capable of taking advantage of the critically or terminally ill, but we do not live in a perfect world. The truth is, there are always unethical individuals who will readily take advantage of those they perceive as physically and/or emotionally weak and vulnerable. They may offer inadequate or unfair settlements that deprive the patient of the full value of his or her life insurance.

While the vast majority of viatical companies and brokers are honest, the need for special control of these activities in dealing with the terminally or critically ill has become important. Several states, while approving the concept of viatical settlements, are taking a closer look at how these settlements are arranged and at the people involved in the process.

This interest has taken the form of legislation introduced for the specific purpose of regulating and overseeing viatical settlements. All states have regulations that insurance companies must conform to, but until now, they have not specifically covered the purchasing of death benefits under a life insurance policy.

The following is a condensed version of such legislation introduced by New York state senator Guy Velella, which was passed and signed into law by Governor Mario Cuomo on August 4, 1993. It is of interest because it reveals the safeguards that may or may not have been imposed in your state but that we all should be familiar with so as to avoid the unscrupulous practices of some companies or individuals.

First, the bill requires that viatical settlement companies and brokers obtain a license from the state insurance department. While some companies are already licensed, the viatical settlement procedure is not technically the same as insurance, and therefore there are organizations and individuals who engage in viatical settlements without a license.

The act provides that:

> No individual, partnership, corporation or other entity may act as a viatical settlement company or broker or enter into or solicit a viatical settlement without first having obtained a license from the Superintendent (of insurance).

The act then specifies the requirements that must be met when obtaining a license from the superintendent, including investigations of the applicants, the fees involved, the process of license renewal, and the issuance of a license to a nonresident applicant. It requires that the names of all members of a corporation, partnership, or other entity be disclosed in the application. Especially important is the provision that requires *designated employees* to be named as well. Even stockholders holding more than five percent of the stock must be named. The purpose, of course, is to give the insurance department the right to investigate any individual involved in the business of soliciting and processing viatical settlements.

The act specifies that the insurance department may revoke, suspend, or refuse to renew a license as a result of any misrepresentation in the license application or any fraudulent or criminal act of the applicant or other violation.

The act requires that the viatical settlement company provide a form of its contract, which the insurance department must approve. In addition, the company must provide the viators with the basic information they are entitled to but are sometimes not given. For example, depending on how the life insurance policy is structured, there could be tax consequences that could work to the disadvantage of the viator. It may still be wise to go ahead with it, but the tax information must be provided at the outset.

Normally, a contract is a contract, and once you sign your name on the dotted line you are bound. But the New York law recognizes the unusually tense and emotional circumstances under which these agreements may be entered into, and therefore provides that the contract may be rescinded by the viator within fifteen days of the receipt of the viatical settlement proceeds. It gives the individual the specific right to have second thoughts—something that can easily happen.

The act protects the viator from delay in payments by

the company—and in some cases, total cessation of payments because of bankruptcy or fraud, or any other possibility. Immediately after the receipt of the documents to effect the transfer of the insurance policy from the viator, the company must pay all of the proceeds to an escrow or trust account managed by a bank approved by the superintendent of insurance. Once the company informs the bank that the transfer of death benefits has taken place, the funds are immediately turned over to the viator.

Every company that is licensed to engage in viatical settlements must file with the insurance department, on or before March 1 of every year, a statement containing information establishing that all regulations have been complied with. The company must make its records, books, and files available to the insurance department for inspection. In the application for the viatical settlement, the company must prominently display the following notice:

> Receipt of payment pursuant to a viatical settlement may affect eligibility for public assistance programs such as medical assistance (Medicaid), aid to families with dependent children, supplementary Social Security income, and AIDS drug assistance programs and may be taxable.

These matters require serious consideration before you enter into a viatical settlement agreement. If other sources of income could be affected, then a decision must be made as to whether the agreement would still be beneficial. In order to be sure, you should consult with the appropriate social service agency concerning how the receipt of funds under a viatical settlement could affect your eligibility, and the eligibility of your spouse and survivors. Also, get a complete breakdown from your tax adviser to determine if there could be any increased liability for federal, state, or local taxes. You may be advised that it would be better to borrow against the policy, so the tax problem will not occur. Every case is different, depending on the numbers, but you must be fully informed about the alternatives before you decide on what would be the best course for you to follow.

The most important aspect of the act is the prohibition of certain unscrupulous activities that some companies or individuals have engaged in when soliciting viatical settlements. The law recognizes that people can be taken advantage of and are vulnerable when making such difficult decisions. For example, the law specifically forbids the communication with any other viatical settlement company or broker of information that discloses financial or other personal confidences. A breach of this confidentiality—making public something that should be communicated to as few people as possible—is not only cruel and insensitive but it also makes the individual vulnerable to nonethical individuals who could use the information for personal profit.

Because of the character—or lack of character—of some who see a gold mine in the viatical settlement business, the law prohibits the payment of a "finder's fee" to anyone who refers the name of a possible viator to any individual or company. Also prohibited is the payment of any compensation to anyone who is not specifically hired as the viator's broker or agent. Remember, the broker's compensation fee does not come from you.

The New York law gives a specific tax break to its citizens who enter into these agreements. The Velella Bill excludes the funds received under viatical settlements from gross income for the purposes of state income tax. (The IRS is not as forgiving and may consider those sums taxable income.)

The act also prohibits any hospital, physician, or nursing home from coercing a patient or resident to enter into a viatical settlement to pay the costs of medical treatment or nursing home care. At the same time, the law prohibits a creditor, even one who has a judgment, from forcing, compelling, or coercing any debtor to enter into a viatical settlement to settle the debt.

The act forbids discrimination in the availability of viatical settlements. In other words, you may not be denied the settlement by companies or individuals on the basis of race, age, sex, national origin, creed, religion, occupation, marital or family status, or whether or not you have dependents.

For those living with terminal illnesses who do not wish to be a financial burden to their families and who wish to maintain their dignity and self-esteem, viatical settlements are appropriate. Rent, health care not covered by insurance, and other essential needs can be covered by the funds received. Companies that purchase death benefits under existing life insurance policies and treat the viators fairly and with understanding and compassion can play an invaluable role.

Nevertheless, there is potential for abuse. The New York statute addresses this potential and sets forth the safeguards that rigidly control activities in viatical settlements. Your state may not have a similar statute, but it is necessary for you to know the ways that you can be taken advantage of and how to avoid them. You must balance the pros and cons of entering into these agreements. Although the assignment of your rights may be the only practical course you can pursue, you must also understand that your beneficiaries will receive nothing —that you have changed the intent of your insurance policy.

Circumstances may leave you no choice but to take this step and assign your death benefits for immediate cash. But do it with your eyes open and be totally informed—about the impact the receipt of this money will have on your other sources of income, about the possible tax consequences, about how to avoid the payment of illegal fees, about the right to change your mind within a reasonable time even after you have entered into the viatical settlement agreement and accepted payment, and about the other considerations referred to here. If your state does not have legislation similar to the New York law, then assert these rights yourself and insist that they be included in your viatical settlement agreement. A responsible company will not object to these reasonable requests. It is not in your best interest to deal with a company that does object.

CHAPTER 8

Living Wills:
Questions and Answers

Generally, the Patient Self Determination Act has acknowledged the rights of the dying. Nevertheless, that law and the applicable cases do not answer all of the questions that arise due to the complexities of the subject. The principle of the right to die may not be complicated, but there are individual day-to-day problems that exist. The following are some questions that are commonly asked concerning advanced directives and procedures.

Q *You mentioned power of attorney, durable power of attorney, and health care proxy. How do the three differ?*

A A *power of attorney* is a written instrument that authorizes another as one's agent. In effect, it gives him or her the right to make decisions for you, and, depending on the nature of the instrument, to enter into agreements. The power of attorney can be drawn for a specific purpose or it can give general and unlimited powers to the agent.

A *durable* power of attorney has a special provision. While the ordinary power of attorney lapses if you, the principal, become incompetent, the durable power remains effective (or in some cases takes effect) if you become incompetent. All fifty states and the District of Columbia have statutes providing for some form of durable power of attorney.

A *health care proxy* is an instrument that designates an agent to make health care decisions for the principal. It may or may not specify the conditions under which life-sustaining medical procedures may be discontinued. These take effect only when and if the principal becomes unable to make his or her own health decisions.

Q *Does the law authorize durable powers of attorney expressly for health care decisions?*

A Yes, there are states that have enacted durable power of attorney statutes to be used expressly for health care decisions, but there are variations from state to state as to the extent of the decision-making power that can be exercised by the agent. Consult the sources that are listed and call for the status in your state.

Q *If my state does not authorize a medical durable power of attorney, can an ordinary durable power of attorney allow the appointment of an agent to make medical decisions?*

A Yes. By your state's court decisions or attorney general decisions, there has been support for the value of executing a durable power of attorney as a way to express your wishes. However, you should clearly state that you intend your agent to make medical decisions.

Q *What are the decisions that my agent must make under a health care proxy?*

A The various states authorize different powers. Depending on your state statute, your agent may be called upon to:

1. Give, withhold, or withdraw consent to specific medical or surgical measures with reference to your condition, prognosis, and known wishes.

2. Authorize end-of-life care, including pain-relieving procedures.

3. Employ, discharge, and give releases to medical personnel.

4. Have access to and disclose medical records.

5. Expend *or withhold* funds needed to carry out medical treatment. (The right to withhold is especially important. It gives your agent authority to inform hospitals, physicians, and other medical personnel that your wishes were that they not proceed with life-sustaining treatment and therefore you or your estate will not be responsible for the expense of such treatment.)

6. Resort to the institution of a legal action, if there is no other alternative, to obtain court authorization regarding decisions about medical treatment.

Q *Whom should I appoint?*

A You can appoint a spouse, relative, or close friend, but the primary requisite is that it must be someone you trust and have complete confidence in. It must be someone who is familiar with your feelings about your medical care in the event that you become terminally ill. You should choose someone who thinks as you do—and supports your ideas and wishes—who will take any and all appropriate action on your behalf, and who is confident about assuming what may be an awesome and even painful responsibility. This appointment must not be made lightly. It will require careful thought and full consultation with your agent.

For safety's sake, consider appointing more than one agent. It is conceivable that the one named may not be available at the time he or she is needed. However, you must specify that only the first agent named is authorized to make the decisions and your "back up" agent is to act only if the first is unavailable.

Q *What issues should I specifically discuss with my agent?*

A When talking about terminal care, you should make perfectly clear your attitudes toward respirators, dialysis, surgery, and all other medical intervention that may only be used to prolong your dying. You should make every effort to understand these medical procedures—what they entail—and what specifically they seek to accomplish. With that knowledge you can more readily specify the particular procedures that you may not wish to be used.

Q *Suppose I have no one to appoint. What do I do then?*
A In that case, execute a living will. While a health
care proxy specifies the individual who will make
the decisions on life-sustaining procedures, the living will puts all health care personnel on notice of
your wishes and is the "clear and convincing" evidence that the courts require to carry out those
wishes. The difference is that the decisions will be
made by medical personnel, family members, or a
court-appointed guardian.

Q *In the event that I have already executed a living will,
can I subsequently appoint an agent to make the decisions.*
A Yes. The two documents reinforce each other, making your wishes and intent even clearer. However,
be certain that the person you choose will make
those important decisions on your behalf, has personal knowledge of your wishes, and fully understands your views and agrees with them.

Q *Are durable powers of attorney and health care proxies
restricted only to situations where my condition is terminal?*
A No. Durable powers of attorney are not usually restricted to terminal conditions and health care
proxies do not have to be. You should discuss your
convictions regarding all medical treatment, not
just the kind that is utilized for the sole purpose of
extending life. Your agent should have the power
to make a wide range of decisions for you, whether
or not your condition is terminal. An advanced

Alzheimer's patient, for example, while not fitting the legal definition of "incompetency," or terminal illness, may be incapable of making informed decisions. These documents also cover situations of temporary incapacity. Accident victims, for example, who will recover, must have medical decisions made during the period of their incapacity.

Q *Reference was made to the Patient Self Determination Act (PSDA) about information that must be given to patients relating to decision-making options. What must be stated to the patient and when?*

A Besides informing patients about their rights to choose or reject medical procedures (as determined by state law and institutional policy), patients must be asked if they have an advanced directive (a living will, health care proxy, or durable power of attorney for health care).

When entering the hospital, the patient must be given information about alternatives, and the details about any existing advance directive should be entered into the patient's record and made part of his or her medical history. Ideally, this should all occur within the first twenty-four hours after admission.

When entering a nursing home, a full discussion of advance planning should occur within the first thirty days of residence. The purpose of this is to have sufficient time to correctly assess the patient's condition, and to build rapport with the patient. If you are the named agent of the patient, discreet inquiry should be made as to whether this discussion has taken place.

In hospice and home health care programs, it is easier to discuss advance directives, because of the relaxed atmosphere. Such discussions could fit in naturally when the nurse or social worker takes the client's medical history as part of an extended first visit.

The time periods referred to are not etched in stone. The law does not set forth time limits within which information must be given and questions asked, but it is fair to say that it must be done within a reasonable time of admission to the institution—and certainly before any relevant decisions have to be made.

Q *What should my health care agent and I discuss when entering into any form of advance directive?*

A Whether you are critically or terminally ill, or currently in good health, you must be as explicit as possible in discussing your thoughts and your views. Don't hold back on anything—discuss the subject thoroughly so that later it cannot be said that you were not explicit as to your intent.

Share all your thoughts about your current health status. If you have critical medical problems, how do they affect your ability to function? Are you being impaired in any way in managing the basic functions of life—eating, sleeping, personal hygiene, etc.?

Discuss your thoughts about your life and if you are satisfied in the way you are living it. What are your positive goals for the future? What do you fear most and what upsets you? Are you independent and self-sufficient? What would your attitude on life-sustaining medical procedures be if you were not able to function in a self-sufficient manner?

What are your religious background and beliefs and how do they affect your views toward actions taken in connection with serious or terminal illness.

Share your perceptions about your physician and medical personnel, including nurses, therapists, chaplains, social workers, etc. Do you have enough faith in your physician to make the final decision about any treatment that may be indicated?

By far the most important subject of discussion should be your attitude toward illness and death, particularly if you are facing terminal illness. This may not be pleasant to think about, much less to discuss, but it is something that must be faced, and it is better to face it calmly and realistically, in a manner that supplies your agent with all of the vital information about you that he or she must know. It is wise to discuss your feelings about the use of life-sustaining measures in the face of imminent death or irreversible coma.

What will be important to you when you are in a terminal state with no hope of recovery? Would you want your family members present? Would you want medication of any kind to reduce your pain? Would you prefer to die in a particular place? Is there something that you would want your agent to do? Would you want to send a message to someone? In other words, is there something left unfinished that you would wish to complete before the book is closed?

Q *If I am to be designated a health care proxy, or an agent under a durable power of attorney, what questions should I ask the principal?*

A You want her or him to be as precise as possible, therefore your questioning must be as thorough as possible. Learn his or her personal values and feelings about what is most important in life, and how religious beliefs would affect decisions. Try to stay away from general questions. For example, "Do you want everything done for you," is much too general and can be subject to various interpretations. Focus instead on specifics, on the practical aspects of medical decisions that could affect the length and the quality of the patient's life. Educate the patient, and if need be, educate yourself about the various medical options that may be available— which of them would be acceptable and which would not.

Q *If I am a patient in one hospital, and I am transferred to another, does the transferring hospital have to provide a copy of my advance directive to the receiving hospital?*

A While the law in your state may not require the document itself to be transferred, the Patient Self Determination Act has been interpreted to mean that the information that you do indeed have an advance directive must be transferred to the new facility. That information is an integral part of your medical record. If a copy of your advance directive was supplied to the original hospital, then it would be prudent for you to request that the document be transferred as well.

Q *Can my wishes be carried out if I don't have a written direction, only oral conversations with a surrogate?*

A Theoretically, testimony of oral conversations can be proof of the "clear and convincing" evidence that is required, but after viewing the experience of the family in the *Elbaum* case, it wouldn't be a safe road to travel. As you will recall, the New York courts in *Elbaum* sent a mixed message. While the testimony of the witnesses was sufficient to prove Mrs. Elbaum's intent, the court also found that the bills incurred, after the husband instructed the nursing home to stop the life-sustaining treatment, had to be paid by Mr. Elbaum. The resistance to oral directives about the cessation of life is constant through the various state court decisions; it is always the burden of the family to prove that the intent to stop life is not just a thought or an idea but a "clear and convincing" intent. If the proof offered through conversations with the patient falls short of meeting that burden, the courts have shown a strong reluctance to order a medical facility to cease and desist from continuing the life-sustaining treatment that had been in force or is proposed.

If you have a specific desire about how you are to be medically treated in the event you become incompetent in a terminally ill condition, then take no chances on oral conversations. Execute an advance directive. If it is clear in its wording, and absent of any irregularities in its execution, it will be honored.

Q *Does the law require that my living will or health care proxy be witnessed, as is required in a last will and testament?*

A Unlike the last will and testament, which requires attesting witnesses in every state, your state may not have any statutory requirement that the living will or health care proxy be witnessed. However, because of the nature of the instrument, you could be looking for trouble by not having it witnessed by at least two people who will sign the document after you sign it in their presence. While it is perfectly natural for you to appoint your spouse, child, or some other close relative as your agent, it is wiser to have nonrelatives sign as witnesses. It is conceivable that even written advance directives could face resistance. For example, an issue may be raised about your competency—your ability to execute such a document—at the time you signed it. Independent witnesses with no stake in your estate would be the most reliable if the instrument was contested in some future litigation.

Q *After the living will or health care proxy is signed, what should I do with the document?*

A First of all, make three or four copies of the original. Give one to your spouse, another to a family member, and a third to a trusted friend or attorney. The more people that are aware of the existence of your advance directive the better. Present the original to the hospital upon admission.

Q *Once I draw up an advance directive, can I change my mind and cancel it, or change the health care agent?*

A You can change your mind at anytime, but if you wish to change your agent, put it in writing in the form of a letter to your agent. Then draw up a new document with the newly named agent and distribute the copies to anyone who had copies of the first. If you wish to nullify the document completely, inform your agent in writing and any others to whom you had distributed copies. If you have named one agent, and you wish to add another—a "back up" in the event that the first is unavailable at the time he or she is needed—then draw up a new document adding the name of the second agent.

CHAPTER 9

Unfinished Business

"Of all the wonders that I have yet heard,
It seems to me most strange that men should fear;
Seeing that death, a necessary end,
Will come when it will come."

In *Julius Caesar,* Shakespeare accurately described the fear of death that besets us all. Yet, in acknowledging the "necessary end," he gives comfort to those who wish to face the approach of death on their own terms.

The law has made great progress in respecting the wishes of those who choose to die with dignity, but it still has a long way to go.

There is still resistance to the wishes of terminally ill patients. In the vast majority of instances, the reason for this is not insensitivity or lack of understanding by the doctor. On the contrary, physicians for the most part are sensitive to the needs and the comfort of their patients. So why the resistance?

The answer lies in the law, which still makes it legally safer for a physician to seek to maintain the life of his patient despite a declared intent to the contrary. He or she is on firmer legal footing to refuse to initiate precise discussions about terminating life, because the law does not shield him or her from a future lawsuit. He or she will not take the chance of overmedicating a patient who is in unbearable and incessant pain because he or she does not want to risk the accusations of hastening the patient's death by using a high dosage of opiates.

If the patient has not executed an advance directive, physicians are aware that they are always subject to second guessing by a member of the family who was not privy to the patient's wishes. There is still the possibility of a lawsuit, even though the patient is suffering intolerable pain and desperately wants to die and the physician knows that all alternatives have been exhausted.

It is unfair to compel the doctor and the patient to play Russian roulette with the law. Naturally, the problem is not so bad if the patient has executed an advance directive, but that is done by relatively few people—only an estimated twenty percent of patients who enter medical facilities. The fact remains that most people depend on oral declarations of their intent. It is my hope that the readers of this book will execute some sort of written advance directive, but if there is none, and suffering becomes intolerable, assisted death should be specifically authorized. All the parties—physicians, guardians, spouses, surrogates, agents, and any others that speak for the patient—should be granted immunity from legal liability after the patient has been certified as being in a terminal condition with no hope of change.

Too many states continue to place rigid and unrealistic prohibitions on doctors and other medical personnel in dealing with patients. While the Patient Self Determination Act has brought us to the point where the right to die is recognized, the interpretation of the law by state courts provides them with little guidance on how to act positively on their own to end the patient's suffering. Despite the very best of intentions, the doctors face the possibility of being named in a malpractice lawsuit. It is no wonder that physicians will not take the chance on being the Good Samaritan, exposing themselves to the legal complications that could besmirch their reputation and wipe them out financially—all for doing the right and humane thing in carrying out their basic purpose.

In the continued absence of a statute granting immunity to doctors and other medical personnel who act in good faith to carry out the patient's wishes, there will be continued hesitancy and resistance by the medical profession. The courts are the last place where these issues should be determined, but under the present state of the law, if you were a physician, your lawyer would be compelled to advise you to end the suffering of the patient only after a court order authorized it.

Some states have moved in a different direction—confusing the issue and placing even more pressures on physicians. Case in point, the so called Kevorkian Law—an antisuicide statute that was hastily enacted to target one person, Dr. Jack Kevorkian, who has openly campaigned for the right to assist suicide and has defied the Michigan legislature that enacted it.

To many, Dr. Kevorkian has become an American folk hero. He has assisted more than nineteen desperate people to end their suffering. He has done this with the determination that it is his moral right, if not his duty, to provide this service. He has brought attention to the suffering of dying people, and has thrown the gauntlet to both the medical and legal professions to take charge of this problem and to deal with it humanely. Right or wrong, he is a man with a mission who is prepared to face imprisonment, actually daring society to punish him for what he firmly believes are his acts of compassion.

Of course, there is another side. Kevorkian's critics call him distressingly arrogant and superficial in his approach to death. They claim that he trivializes the act of helping another human being to die—the most profound of human decisions. They claim also that he is a publicity seeker—that there is more focus on his suicide machines and his personality than on the plight of his patients and that he is merely seeking a quick fix to a complex human problem.

Perhaps some of these criticisms are valid. He does not have an ingratiating style and may not treat the subject with the appropriate solemnity that it calls for. He may not be the best spokesman for his point of view. But Kevorkian has served a purpose. His well-publicized actions have focused public attention on those who do not want to survive in intolerable pain with no hope of recovery and who seek out help to end an existence that they cannot cope with—emotionally or physically. Most important, he has forced the public to contemplate that "those people" could very well be "us" by a turn of fate or circumstance.

If the various legislatures and courts throughout the nation took a more tolerant view of those who want to exercise their right to die in the face of the pain of an incurable and irreversible physical condition, there would be no need for Kevorkian. Those nineteen people sought him out because they believed they had no other place to turn. The harsh Michigan statute has placed a chilling effect on efforts to provide more compassionate medical assistance to the dying. The thrust of the statute, which made it a crime to "assist suicide," is so vague that it could very well cause a physician to think twice about any assistance to the dying that could result in a peaceful death.

Other alternatives should be explored. For example, hospice care can offer a sensitive course for the dying. Ideally, the terminally ill can be at home, or in a home-like setting, with the participation of nurses, members of the clergy, and family members. State financing of hospice care would give those who face imminent death the security of knowing that they can die with some comfort and sense of control.

The bottom line is dignity. When suffering becomes intolerable or when comatose patients breathe only with mechanical assistance, the law should recognize the absolute right of a loved one or a surrogate to make the decision to terminate life. Moreover, the law should protect all the parties involved from any liability.

Cruzan and later cases have opened the door to exercising the right to choose. They are steps in the right direction, but society needs to make further progress. We do not trivialize life; we must not trivialize death. Until we show the same respect for both, Kevorkian and other people like him are our only alternatives.

CHAPTER 10

The Canadian Position

Canada has not come as far as the U.S. in recognizing the right to die with dignity. Nevertheless, there are active organizations which are vigorously pursuing the same goals as Choice in Dying, Inc., in the U.S. Two such groups, the Right to Die Society of Canada, and Dying with Dignity, were intervenors in a recently decided case by the Supreme Court of Canada. While the resulting determination by the Court was not favorable to their position, a close scrutiny of the language used by the court, and the manner in which it ruled, gives rise to hope for future progress.

The court ruled that the appellant did *not* have the right to choose her means of death. Since that is the ruling of the Supreme Court of Canada, it is therefore the law of the land—right now. Let us examine, however, the encouraging factors that emerged from the case which hold out the possibility that Canadians will be granted what Americans now possess—the right to choose.

First, and very significantly, the court decided the issue by the slimmest majority. Of the nine judges of the Canadian Supreme Court, four dissented, *including the Chief Justice,* and filed opinions which upheld the patient's right to choose.

Second, by reading the case closely, it appears that the dissenting judges could very well have picked up that one deciding vote had the facts been slightly changed. Let us review the Rodriguez case, decided by the Supreme Court of Canada in August of 1993.

Sue Rodriguez v. The Attorney General of Canada and the Attorney General of British Columbia

Sue Rodriguez was a 42 year old mother suffering from ALS, amyotrophic lateral sclerosis. It is commonly known as Lou Gehrig's disease, a horribly debilitating malady resulting in total muscle deterioration. At the time she commenced court proceedings, her condition was worsening. She would soon lose the ability to swallow, speak, walk and move her body without assistance. She would be unable to breathe without a respirator, and to eat without the insertion of a gastrostomy tube. There was no prognosis for improvement, only total deterioration. Her life expectancy at the time of the court's decision was between 2 to 14 months.

Sue Rodriguez did not wish to die as long as she had the capacity to enjoy life. Nevertheless, being aware of the brief time remaining, she requested that a qualified physician be allowed to set up technological means by which she might, *by her own hand,* at the time of her choosing, end her life. Concededly, this would violate Section 241 of the Criminal Code which provides:

> Every one who (a) counsels a person to commit suicide, or (b) aids or abets a person to commit suicide, whether suicide ensues or not, is guilty of an indictable offence and liable to imprisonment for a term not exceeding fourteen years. (Note the similarity to the Michigan anti-Kevorkian Law.)

When the physicians understandably refused to comply with her request under constraints of the statute, she applied to the Supreme Court of British Columbia for an order declaring Section 241 to be invalid. She set forth as her grounds that the statute violated her rights as described under Section 7 of the Canadian Charter of Rights and Freedoms,* which reads:

> 7. Every one has the right to life, liberty and security of the person and the right not to be deprived thereof except in accordance with the principles of fundamental justice

Sue Rodriguez saw the statute as a source of rights deprivation because it interfered with her ability to live her remaining life with the inherent dignity of a human person. She also maintained that she had the absolute right to be free of governmental interference in making fundamental personal decisions concerning the terminal stages of her life.

---

* The charter of Rights and Freedoms is similar to the American Bill of Rights which guarantees basic rights to its citizens.

The majority opinion rested largely on the sanctity of life. One of the judges wrote that such sanctity excludes freedom of choice in the self-infliction of death, and that the state has the absolute right to regulate the involvement of others in exercising power over individuals ending their lives. In asserting that there could be no exceptions, the judge stated:

> Death is, for all mortals, inevitable. Even when death appears imminent, seeking to control the manner and timing of one's death constitutes a conscious choice of death over life.

It was his position then, that in the case of a terminally ill patient with no hope of recovery, even when he or she is non-functioning or in unbearable pain, the value of extending life must prevail.

Canadian judges apparently have followed the Kevorkian case with great interest. Another member of the court who apparently was greatly concerned by the possibility of Kevorkians spreading like wild mushrooms all through Canada, wrote:

> Since much of the medical profession is opposed to being involved in assisting suicide because it is antithetical to their roles as healers of the sick, many doctors will refuse to assist, leaving open the potential for the growth of a macabre specialty in this area reminiscent of Dr. Kevorkian and his suicide machine.

The minority opinion, in my view, was more cogent and relevant, concentrating on the specific rights of Sue

Rodriguez, instead of the philisophical concepts of the morality of choice. Their opinion was that she was being denied a choice available to others, and that such deprivation could not be justified. They made the point that Parliament made suicide lawful but assisted suicide unlawful. As one judge expressed it:

> The effect of this distinction is to deny to some people the choice of ending their lives solely because they are physically unable to do so, preventing them from exercising the autonomy over their bodies available to other people. The denial of the ability to end their life is arbitrary and hence amounts to a limit on the right to security of the person which does not comport with the principles of fundamental justice.

The minority stressed the point that fundamental justice requires that each person, *considered individually,* be treated fairly by the law. The language was clear and explicit:

> I can see no difference between permitting a patient of sound mind to choose death with dignity by refusing treatment and permitting a patient of sound mind who is terminally ill to choose death with dignity by terminating life preserving treatment, even if, because of incapacity, that step has to be physically taken by another on her instructions. Nor can I see any reason for failing to extend that same permission so that a terminally ill patient facing death may put an end to her life through the intermediary of another, as suggested by Sue Rodriguez. The right to choose death is open to patients who

are not physically handicapped. There is no reason for denying that choice to those who are.

The dissenters took issue with the position of the majority which held the sanctity of life to be superior to the rights of the terminally ill. They described with commanding logic that such is not the case:

> Section 7 of the Canadian Charter of Rights and Freedoms has granted the constitutional right to Canadians to life, liberty, and the security of the person. It is a provision which emphasizes the innate dignity of human existence. The life of an individual must include dying. Dying is the final act in the drama of life.

The well-reasoned rationale was that dying is an integral part of living, and as a part of life it is entitled to constitutional protection. In other words, the right to die with dignity should be as well protected as is any other aspect of the right to life, and that any state laws or regulations which would force a dreadful and painful death on an incapacitated terminally ill patient is an affront to human dignity.

The encouraging aspect of the *Rodriguez* case is that it traces the history of the American evolvement in securing the rights of the terminally ill. The *Cruzan* case led to the passage of the Patient Self Determination Act because the U.S. Congress was alerted to the determination of U.S. citizens to sanction the right to choose. The dissent in the *Rodriguez* case opens the door to similar legislation in Canada. One of the judges referred to "the failure of Parliament to address the problem of the terminally ill." It is reasonable to assume that the sentiments of four out of nine judges speaks for at least the same proportion of Canadians. As more citizens give thought to the serious implications of the right to choose, Parliament will have to address the subject because it is an issue that won't go away.

It is significant that the majority opinion appeared to be greatly concerned with the fact that Sue Rodriguez needed the intervention of another to be "physically taken." Such action would of course violate Section 241. But let us assume that Sue Rodriguez had limited her request to the cessation of life-sustaining treatment. Based on the tenor of the opinions written by the majority, it is highly conceivable that such a request would not be viewed as the intervention of another—and therefore would not be a violation of the statute. Concededly, this is a fine distinction, but a criminal statute must be strictly construed. Under the latter circumstances, the act of terminating her life would be Sue Rodriguez's and not anyone else's.

The most encouraging factor for Canadians who seek the same rights afforded Americans under the Patient Self Determination Act was the astute dissenting opinion by Chief Justice Antonio Lamar. He came to grips with the Draconian aspect of the "assisted suicide" law as it applied to Sue Rodriguez and others similarly situated. By siding with the minority, he in fact ruled that the statute violated her human rights. But Judge Lamar went further. Recognizing that the statute had a favorable objective, he proposed that "constitutional exemptions" be made available to Sue Rodriguez and others in her circumstances. Among his proposals were:

(a) That her request should be complied with after she had been certified by a treating physician and independent psychiatrist to be competant to make the decision to end her own life.

(b) That the physicians must certify that she had made her decision freely and voluntarily, and at least one of the physicians must be present with her at the time she commits assisted suicide.

(c) The physicians must also certify that she is or will become physically incapable of committing suicide unassisted, and that she has been informed, and understands, that she has a continuing right to change her mind about terminating her life.

(d) She must be examined daily by one of the certifying physicians.

(e) The *act* causing her death must be hers alone, and not of anyone else.

Obviously, this case differs from the American examples which involved requests by the patient to have others refrain from continuing treatment. It's object, however, is the same—to attain death with dignity.

Hopefully, for the benefit of all who may face the torment of Sue Rodriguez, the Canadian Parliament will look at the proposals by Judge Lamar very closely, and incorporate them into legislation which will be more realistic and compassionate. Although the court, by a slim majority, found the law did not violate Section 7 of the Charter of Rights and Freedoms, the logic of Lamar's suggested amendments is commanding.

LIVING WILL FORM

I,_____, being of sound mind, make this statement as a directive to be followed if I become permanently unable to participate in decisions regarding my medical care. These instructions reflect my firm and settled commitment to decline medical treatment under the circumstances indicated below:

I direct my attending physician to withhold or withdraw treatment that serves only to prolong the process of my dying, if I should be in an *incurable or irreversible mental or physical condition with no reasonable expectation of recovery.*

These instructions apply if I am (a) *in a terminal condition;* (b) *permanently unconscious;* or (c) *if I am conscious but have irreversible brain damage and will never regain the ability to make decisions and express my wishes.*

I direct that treatment be limited to measures to keep me comfortable and to relieve pain, including any pain that might occur by withholding or withdrawing treatment.

While I understand that I am not legally required to be specific about future treatments, *if I am in the condition(s) described above I feel especially strongly about the following forms of treatment:*

I do not want cardiac resuscitation.

I do not want mechanical respiration.

I do not want tube feeding.

I do not want antibiotics.

I do want maximum relief.

Other directions (insert personal instructions):_____

_____

_____

(continued)

These directions express my legal right to refuse treatment, under the law of New York. I intend my instructions to be carried out, unless I have rescinded them in a new writing or by clearly indicating that I have changed my mind.

Signed: _____   Date: _____

Witness: _____

Address: _____

_____

_____

Keep the signed original with your personal papers at home. Give copies of the signed original to your doctor, family, lawyer and others who might be involved in your care.

HEALTH CARE PROXY FORM

(1) I,_____hereby appoint _____
                                   (name, address and phone number)
_____ as my health care agent to
make any and all health care decisions for me, except to the
extent that I state otherwise. This proxy shall take effect when
and if I become unable to make my own health care decisions.

(2) Optional instructions: I direct my proxy to make health care
decisions in accord with my wishes and limitations as stated
below, or as he or she otherwise knows. (Attach additional
pages if necessary).
(NOTE: Unless your agent knows your wishes about artificial
nutrition and hydration [feeding tubes], your agent will not
be allowed to make decisions about artificial nutrition and
hydration.)

(3) Name of substitute or fill-in proxy if the person I appoint
above is unable, unwilling or unavailable to act as my health
care agent. (optional)

_____

(Name)

_____

(Substitute's home address and telephone number)

(4) Unless I revoke it, this proxy shall remain in effect indefinitely, or until the date or conditions stated below. This proxy
shall expire (specific date or conditions, if desired)_____

(5) _____

(Your Signature)

_____

(Your Address)

_____

(Date)

(continued)

STATEMENT BY WITNESSES (MUST BE 18 OR OLDER)

I declare that the person who signed this document is personally known to me and appears to be of sound mind and acting of his or her own free will. He or she signed (or asked another to sign for him or her) this document in my presence.

Witness 1_____ Address_____

Witness 2_____ Address_____

DURABLE POWER OF ATTORNEY (MEDICAL)

I,_____, of the County of_____State of_____hereby appoint_____as my attorney-in-fact, giving my attorney-in-fact power to do the following:

To make any arrangements that are appropriate and in my best interests relating to my medical or dental care.

To give or withhold consent in my name to any and all types of medical treatment or surgical procedures.

To give or withhold consent in my name to the disclosure of any confidential or privileged communication or information relating to my medical condition, and to sign, acknowledge and deliver in my name any documents necessary to carry out the authority granted to my attorney-in-fact in this document.

To make any and all health care decisions for me.

This is intended to be a **DURABLE POWER OF ATTORNEY.** *It shall continue to be in effect in the event of my disability or incapacity which would render me unable to make my own health care decisions.*

IN WITNESS WHEREOF, I have executed this Power of Attorney this ___ day of _____, 199___.

_____

(Your Signature)

(continued)

ATTESTATION

We hereby certify that his/her Power of Attorney was signed, declared and published by_____as his/her Power of Attorney on this day, in our presence and in the presence of each other, and we sign our names below as witnesses in his/her presence, at his/her request, and the presence of each other on the ___ day of _____, 199___.

_____   _____
Witness 1 Signature   Residing at

_____   _____
Witness 2 Signature   Residing at

State of _____

County of _____

On this ___ day of _____, 199___, before me, the undersigned, a Notary Public in and for the State and County above named, personally appeared, _____ who is known to me personally to be the principal described in and who executed the above Power of Attorney, and after first being sworn, declared this instrument as his/her free act and deed and signed it in my presence.

Subscribed and sworn to before me this ___ day of _____, 199___.

_____
(Seal Affixed)   Notary Public

Note: This is an example of a Durable Power of Attorney designed for the special purpose of making health care decisions. Normally, powers of attorneys are not so limited, and grant agents many more powers. The wording contained herein can be used to supplement the other powers if you wish the document to be more inclusive.

WILLS

AND TRUSTS

Introduction

Wills and Trusts

If you are lucky, you will live your life from birth to death without requiring the services of a lawyer. However, a lawyer may be indispensable at the time of your death.

It is wise for *everyone* to make a will—the reasons for this will be set forth. You definitely need a lawyer for a will, or at least to consult with one about its form. And after your death, an attorney will represent the executor who has been named in the will to manage your estate. If you neglected to make a will, an attorney will have to represent the administrator of the estate, someone appointed by the court to manage your estate because you died intestate—without a will—and no executor was named.

Lawyers are expensive. You already know that. The purpose of Part II of this book is to give you an insight into the subject of wills, trusts, and estates so that you can march into your lawyer's office with the capacity to make informed decisions about the important issues facing you and your family.

Knowledge is power—the power to have a firmer control over your life and, after you've gone, the lives of your loved ones. Knowledge may also help you cut down on legal fees. It certainly isn't desirable for you to enter your lawyer's office and receive a law school course at the rate of $250 per hour. It is better, and far less expensive, for you to be prepared with a rough draft of the document you wish to execute (samples of which are included in this book) and say, "Counselor, this is what I want to be done. Correct any part of it that you believe does not suit my purpose, but alter it, or any part of it, only if you have to."

You will be happily surprised at how much can be saved by having an educated concept of why you are visiting the attorney in the first place.

Yes, wills, trusts, and estates are complicated subjects, but not so complicated that they are incomprehensible. My purpose here is to reduce the complexities so that they can be understood in everyday shirt-sleeve English. The words that lawyers use, which tend to mystify, can be defined and simplified. Lawyers charge by the hour, and sometimes by the word. Sometimes the fees are increased in proportion to the syllables! You will be at a distinct advantage if you comprehend the attorney's frame of reference.

What you read here will not qualify you for a law degree, but it will help you understand what your lawyer is talking about.

Chapter 11

Basic Principles

What is a will? A will is a written instrument by an adult (in most states a person over the age of eighteen). It directs how the property of the deceased is to be disposed. It also can direct how not to dispose of the property. The will designates the person or persons who will have the necessary power and authority to carry out the stated wishes contained in it.

What is a testator? The testator (or testatrix if a woman) is the person who makes the will. His or her property will be disposed of only according to the terms and conditions contained in the will and will be distributed pursuant to those terms and conditions after his or her death.

What is an executor? An executor (or executrix if a woman) is the party named in the will by the testator who has been given the power, duty, and authority to carry out the written intentions of the testator. The powers of the executor can be unlimited, or may be limited for specific purposes. The testator may name more than one executor who can act jointly with the other. Provision can also be made for an alternate executor in the event the first named executor dies before the testator.

Can there be an oral will? Yes, but it will be accepted in limited circumstances. No writing is involved, but it must be clearly established by two witnesses. It is called a *nuncupative will.*

There is another type of will that is also legal under the same limited circumstances. It is written entirely in the handwriting of the testator. No witnesses are required. This is called a *holographic will.*

When are nuncupative or holographic wills valid? Only when made by:

A. A member of the armed forces while in military or naval service during a war or other armed conflict in which members of the armed forces are engaged. (This does not require a formal declaration of war.)

B. A person who serves with or accompanies an armed force engaged in actual military or naval service during such war or other armed conflict. (This includes journalists, Red Cross workers, government officials, and any and all others who are present.)

C. A mariner at sea.

Both nuncupative and holographic wills become invalid after:

A. One year from the date of discharge of a member of the armed forces.
B. One year from the date that the person ceases to accompany the armed forces.
C. Three years from the date that the will was made by a mariner at sea.

Must a will have a specific structure or form? No. A will can be handwritten, typewritten, or printed on a legal form usually found in legal stationers.

What is a codicil? A codicil is a clause or supplement that is added to a will. It can partially revoke, alter, or confirm any of the provisions. However, you cannot totally revoke a will by adding a codicil.

How do I revoke a will? A will is revoked in its entirety by destroying it physically or by executing a subsequent will. When you revoke a will, you revoke all prior codicils as well.

Does the law require that the testator sign his or her full name?

While the will must be signed by the testator, initials could be a valid signature. An illiterate person can execute a will by signing with his or her mark, such as an X. If the testator is too weak to sign, he or she can be helped to affix his or her signature. A third person can sign for the testator under the testator's direction and in the testator's presence as long as that third person also signs in the presence of two others, who must sign as witnesses.

Where must the signature appear? The testator's signature *must be at the end of the will.* Anything that is added after or below the signature of the testator is totally invalid. In one case, a testator used both sides of a 3″ × 5″ index card. He wrote his signature on the margin, perpendicularly to the contents of the card. The witnesses signed on the back. The attempted will was denied probate (held invalid) because the testator's signature "was not at the end thereof."

This rule is strictly enforced. Take the case of the careless lawyer. He, or someone in his office, inadvertently stapled page three of the will after page four and offered it for probate. Unfortunately, the testator's signature appeared on page four. All of the provisions appearing on page three were disallowed because as the will was presented to the probate judge, they appeared *after* the testator's signature.

What is the legal role of the witnesses? For a will to be valid, there must be at least two witnesses to the testator's signing. (Check the number required in your state). They must sign the document in the presence of the testator. The testator must declare to them that the document he or she has signed is his or her last will and testament.

If a will is contested, the witnesses must be prepared to testify that they saw the testator sign it or that the testator acknowledged that it was his or her signature.

Normally, a will contains an *attestation clause,* a statement by the witnesses in which they attest to the regularity of the procedure. The following is a typical attestation clause:

This instrument was signed by *John Jones,* the testator, at the end of the will, and in the presence of us or acknowledged to us that this was his signature and that this was declared to be his last will and testament, and we thereupon subscribed our names as witnesses at his request and in his presence.

The date and the signature of the witnesses follow this clause. The attestation clause is inserted as a safeguard against any future contest to the will or the manner in which it was executed. However, the absence of the attestation clause will not invalidate the will provided that the two witnesses have signed.

Can a beneficiary under a will (one who has been named to receive money or other property) be a subscribing witness?

The will itself is not voided, but if one of the witnesses is an "interested witness," (one who would inherit under the terms of the will), the disposition of that *benefit* would be voided and the rest of the will would stay in tact. However, if at the time of the execution of the will there are two other disinterested witnesses (those that would not receive anything under the terms of the will) who have signed, then the entire will would remain enforceable. (Again, this depends on the number of witnesses that your state requires.)

There is another circumstance where the beneficiary would not be deprived of his or her legacy. That occurs when the beneficiary is an *intestate distributee* (a person whom the law says would have a right to inherit if the testator had died without a will.) The rights of intestacy will be explained later in further detail.

Try to avoid having a recipient under your will sign as a subscribing witness. It can cause other complications, such as possible claims of duress by a disgruntled relative who was left out. The object in drawing a will is to make it as invulnerable to attack as possible. Intrafamily squabbles about the estate of the deceased often get messy.

May an executor, trustee, or guardian named in the will to carry out the written directions of the testator also be a witness?

There is no prohibition against an executor, trustee, guardian, or any other fiduciary named in the will from acting as a subscribing witness, as long as that individual is not also named as a party who will receive a legacy under the terms of the will. The fact that he or she may receive compensation for his or her duties does not affect his or her validity as a witness.

What is the procedure if the witnesses to the signing of the will cannot be located?

A. If one witness is missing, or cannot testify because of death, incompetency, absence from the state, or inability to be found within the jurisdiction, the probate judge has the discretion to allow the will into probate based on the testimony of just one witness. If the witness is outside the state but cannot or will not return, the judge may order his or her testimony to be taken by deposition.

B. If both witnesses are missing, dead, or outside the state, it naturally becomes more difficult to have the will admitted to probate. The laws of the different states vary as to how this can be done. In some jurisdictions, the judge is authorized by law to admit the will based on proof of the testator's handwriting and proof of at least one witness's handwritten signature, together with other evidence submitted to prove the propriety of the will.

Some jurisdictions follow the "ancient document" rule, which holds that if a document is found that is thirty years old (the amount of years varies from state to state) and its appearance and location when found does not raise suspicion, the court may allow it as an "ancient document," and in the case of a will, it would not need the required proof of the validity of the testator's signature or of the witnesses. It must be said, however, that it is extremely difficult to prove a will in that way.

There is a precaution that one can take to protect against the possibility of not having the witnesses available when the will is submitted for probate by the executor. Normally, the testator's signature is not notarized, nor are the witnesses. However, many attorneys have the witnesses sign affidavits of subscribing witnesses, which are sworn notarized statements setting forth all the elements that the judge will look for in admitting the will for probate when the witnesses are not available to testify. A form of such an affidavit follows. I recommend that it be used in the drawing of every will, regardless of whether the witnesses are close relatives or friends.

AFFIDAVIT OF SUBSCRIBING WITNESSES

State of _____

County of _____

_____ and _____,
each of the undersigned, deposes and says:

The within will was subscribed in our presence and sight at the end thereof by JOHN JONES, the within named testator on the _____ day of _____, 19 _____ at *(designate place)*.

Said testator at the time of making such subscription declared the instrument to be his Last Will and Testament.

Each of the undersigned thereupon signed his name as a witness at the end of said Will, at the request of said Testator and in his presence and in the presence and the sight of each other.

Said Testator was, at the time of so executing said Will, over the age of 18 years and, in the respective opinions of the undersigned, of sound mind, memory, and understanding and not under any restraint or in any respect incompetent to make a Will.

Said Testator, in the respective opinions of the undersigned, could read, write, and converse in the English language and was suffering from no defect of sight, hearing, or speech, or from any other physical or mental impairment which would affect his capacity to make a valid Will. This Will was executed as a single, original instrument and was not executed in counterparts.

Each of the undersigned was acquainted with said Testator at such time and makes this affidavit at his request. The subscription, declaration and attestation was supervised by an attorney.

_____

_____

_____

Severally subscribed and
sworn to before me this
_____ day of _____, 19 _____

_____
Notary Public

Q *The will is made. The testator dies. The family knows that it was in his possession, but after his death it is not found among his belongings. Does this mean the will can't be offered for probate?*

A Not always. While it is true that there is a presumption under the law that if the will is not found the testator had destroyed it, that presumption is rebuttable, meaning that the court could allow it to be probated if its nonproduction can be explained by competent and credible evidence. For example, let us assume that he gave it to his attorney for safe keeping, and the attorney for some reason cannot produce it, through loss or inadvertant destruction. The will can still be admitted to probate if:

1. It can be established, through the attorney and/or others that the will has not been revoked by the testator. (While it is extremely difficult to prove a negative, persuasive evidence could cause the court to make that finding.)

2. The will is proved to be validly executed.

3. *All of the provisions* of the will are proved by the testimony of two witnesses. They need not necessarily be subscribing witnesses, but that of course would be preferable.

(Note: These are sample lost will procedures, used by New York and other jurisdictions. Check with your local counsel for the sources listed for the law in your state.)

CHAPTER 12

Beneficiaries

Despite a will that is validly executed, not lost, and clearly states the testator's wishes, there are instances where the beneficiary may be unable to take the property because of actions taken by himself, the testator, or both.

The following are some examples:

A. The testator, John Jones, names his nephew Sam Smith as a beneficiary. However, anticipating that his nephew may not be too happy with the amount left to him, the testator inserts a "no contest" clause. This says that if any beneficiary under the will contests the will for any reason, the objector will lose his or her inheritance. Nevertheless, the nephew contests the will. If he fails in the contest, he could lose it all.

B. The testator, John Jones, had, during his lifetime, entered into a contract with Fred Clark. In a written document, he promises Clark that in consideration for certain work done by Clark for Jones during his lifetime, Jones will make him an heir for a specified amount of money or property. This is an enforceable contract and all of Fred Clark's promised legacy must be paid first—even if it leaves insufficient or no funds to pay Sam Smith's legacy.

C. John Jones gives, and Sam Smith accepts, a gift during life that is intended as an advancement to satisfy the share that Sam Smith would otherwise receive at the death of the testator. The beneficiary cannot receive it twice. Normally, that situation can be taken care of if the testator adds a codicil explaining why the bequest has been eliminated or if a new will is drawn. However, we sometimes forget these details.

D. Sam Smith owes a sum of money to John Jones that was never paid. The executor can take the position that this debt can be "set off" against the bequest given to Sam Smith and refuse to honor that part of it, or all of it if the debt equals or exceeds the bequest.

E. The Case of the Murdering Beneficiary. This is a common theme in TV movies. The basic plot is that the beneficiary under a will does not want to wait for the testator's death and helps the testator to his final end. You would think that the murderer would not be able to collect on his or her ill-gotten gains. But that is not always the case. Some states have specific laws that prevent a beneficiary from receiving anything under a will if he or she is involved in the murder of the testator. But some do not, and if the law is silent about it, in some jurisdictions courts permit the murdering beneficiary to collect, even though he or she is locked away in a place where they can't enjoy it. In the end, if the legislatures are silent about depriving the murdering beneficiary of his or her bequest, the courts cannot write the law, although common sense dictates that they should.

Finally, the courts have found a way to do the right thing. In many states, the inheritance of the murderer goes into a "constructive trust" for the benefit of persons who "otherwise would have received the property." This is what lawyers call a verbal fiction, a device to achieve the same effect as if the inheritance or bequest was denied to the murderer. One way or another, the modern approach is the old common law maxim— "No man shall be permitted to profit by his own wrong."

Rights of Heirs under Intestacy

If the deceased has made no will, he has died intestate. This state of intestacy triggers laws that govern the distribution of estates. Under the old common law, there were certain "natural" heirs who would receive portions of the estate as their right. That concept is still recognized, except that various states have devised their own legal definitions of natural heirs and the shares or percentage of the estate each heir is entitled to. The chart below sets forth the method of distribution under New York law. It is displayed only as an example of how a state can devise its own rules of distribution. We have said many times that you must consult local counsel or refer to the sources of information we have listed to be informed of the precise law in your state. That is especially important on the subject of intestacy, where states vary in many ways. Heirs in some states cannot be heirs in others, and the percentage of the distribution can be quite different.

When reading this chart, keep in mind that the property referred to does not apply to property that may pass to the spouse by operation of law and therefore is not considered disposable property. For example, if a husband and wife own a house in both their names, they are what is referred to as tenants by the entirety. Upon the death of one, the other receives all rights, title, and interest to the property outright, and this is not affected by the laws of inheritance. In other words, the property is not part of the deceased's estate. It goes directly to the surviving spouse "by operation of law." The same may be true of joint bank accounts, or any other property that the husband and wife own jointly and have provided that the survivor takes all. This also applies to life insurance benefits and pensions. They are not part of the estate.

You will also see from the chart that in certain instances a parent can inherit from a child. However, where a parent has abandoned a child, the parent loses the right to inherit, but a child who has been abandoned never loses the right to inherit.

DISTRIBUTION OF PROPERTY WHEN DECEDENT HAS NOT MADE A WILL

Decedent survived by	Distributive share
Spouse and children	$50,000 and $1/2$ of the balance to spouse, remainder to children
Spouse and no children	Everything to spouse
Children and no spouse	Everything to children
One or both parents, and no spouse and no children	Everything to parent or parents
Siblings and no spouse, children, or parent	Everything to siblings

Note: These are partial provisions from the New York Intestacy Law, which apply to all estates where the deceased died after September 1, 1992.

Right of Election

If the deceased spouse does not provide for the surviving spouse, or if the provision is inadequate, the law steps in and grants the surviving spouse a specified amount. That is commonly referred to as the widow's right of election (although it can be equally asserted by the widower). All states have some form of right to election, with various minimum amounts or percentages of the estate that the surviving spouse may claim. Here is how it works in New York.

Assume that the husband dies leaving an estate of $100,000 and provides in his will that his wife receive $40,000. The New York law says that that is not enough. She is entitled, by statute, to receive $50,000 or one third of the net estate, whichever is greater.

She naturally exercises her right of election and chooses to receive the sum of $50,000 in place of the $40,000 that was given to her in the will.

A spouse, prior to or during a marriage, can agree to waive the right of election or drastically limit it by written instrument. For example, the parties can enter into a prenuptual agreement, which is a contract made before marriage wherein the two parties agree on a set amount that the wife will receive in the event of divorce or death of the husband. This is an enforceable contract if voluntarily made and if, in the agreement, the widow has specifically waived (released and/or given up) her right to election, the amount specified in that agreement is the amount she will receive.

The right of election is a personal right, meaning that only she can exercise it. However, if she had been adjudicated an incompetent at the time of her husband's death, then her guardian or committee can elect on her behalf. Also, if the surviving spouse is an infant, the guardian can exercise the right of election on his or her behalf.

Examples related here of right of election of surviving spouse have referred to the widow, because that is the most common circumstance. However, the surviving spouse can of course be the husband, and the same rules and examples apply.

Where a surviving spouse elects against an estate, he or she receives his or her share outright, and all other legatees (recipients) contribute to the increase.

Exempt Property

There is certain property that is not considered part of the estate for intestate or right of election purposes. In other words, this property goes directly to the widow or widower or, if there is none, to children under the age of twenty-one years. The following property is exempt under the New York statute:

1. Personal property of the deceased up to $5000
2. The contents of a library up to $500
3. The value of decedent's automobile up to $10,000
4. $1000 in cash

As with other specifics in statutes, exempt property and the amounts vary from state to state. Consult with counsel about what is considered exempt property in your state.

Domicile

The widow has the right of election concerning property that was owned by the deceased *in the state where he was domiciled*. Domicile has been defined as being "that place where a person has a true, fixed, and permanent home, for an unlimited and indefinite period." You can see by the definition that the concept is subject to interpretation, and many lawsuits concern themselves with such interpretations. There has been endless litigation about the difference between a residence, which could be temporary, and a domicile, which connotes permanency. The right of election does not extend to the real property (land) of the decedent outside the State of New York. At the same time, if the widow is not domiciled in the same state where the real property is located, the right of election may not be available to her.

There is a time limit in exercising the right of election. When an executor submits a will for probate, the judge issues what is referred to as *letters testamentary*, which then gives him or her the power and authority to proceed to carry out his or her duties, such as marshaling the assets, paying the creditors, and seeing to it that each of the named distributees receives his or her share.

When a person dies intestate, an application is made by someone, usually a close relative, to exercise the same duties and distribute the assets according to that particular jurisdiction's laws on intestacy. The person appointed by the court is called the administrator (administratrix if a woman) who is issued *letters of administration*.

If the surviving spouse wants to exercise the right of election, she (or he) must make written notification to the executor or administrator within a specified time from the date of issuance of the *letters testamentary* or the *letters of administration*. In New York, the time limit is six months, but the court has discretion to allow the election to be filed within twelve months. Check the time limit in your state, but remember that if the statutory period expires, the right of election will also. The courts will not allow the surviving spouse to "sleep on her rights."

The right of election guarantees the widow a specified amount. The proceeds of a life insurance policy where she is named the beneficiary go directly to her. Those sums are not computed as part of the estate if she should assert her right of election.

For example, let us assume that the husband who executed a will left an estate of $100,000, but in addition he had purchased a life insurance policy with the face value of $50,000, naming his wife as beneficiary. The proceeds of the policy go directly to her. Her right of election is directed to the assets of the estate ($100,000), and she can receive that statutory minimum amount in addition to the money received as beneficiary of the policy.

However, for right of election purposes only, the same may not apply to joint bank accounts. In some jurisdictions, at least for state tax purposes, the deceased's half does become part of the estate. Pension or profit-sharing proceeds may or may not revert to the estate, depending upon how they are structured.

Where no will exists, it is safe to say that the probate process can be avoided when a joint instrument is drawn (such as a joint bank account) and the survivor takes all. So why not just place everything in both names, period? We'll discuss the pros and cons of that later.

CHAPTER 13

Events Occurring After the Will Is Signed

After the testator makes a valid will, there are certain events that may occur afterward that could affect the terms of the will. The following are some of them:

A. *Testator marries.* If the surviving spouse is not mentioned in the will at the time of its signing, and the testator married after he signed it, the surviving spouse has the right of election to claim his or her share which is authorized by statute. It makes no difference when they married, as long as the marriage was valid and the state of marriage existed between them at the time of the testator's death.

B. *After born children.* This refers to *all children* conceived by the testator after the will is signed, in and out of wedlock, and also includes adopted children. Several states provide that if the testator had no child living when he or she executed his or her will, the after born children are entitled to share in the estate.

C. *Divorce or annulment.* If the testator's marriage is dissolved by divorce or annulment after the will is drawn, and signed, the bequest to the surviving spouse is no longer valid. However, if the parties remarry, the remarriage revives the bequests to the spouse and he or she can receive them under the terms of the existing will.

If after the divorce, the testator adds a codicil to his will that reinstates the bequest to his former wife, she will be entitled to receive the bequest even though she was not married to the testator at the time of his death.

If a divorced spouse is named as a beneficiary in an insurance policy before the divorce, she, unlike the case of being named in a will, would *not* lose her benefits. The only exception to that rule, in some jurisdictions, is when she is found guilty of adultery.

Unlike a divorce, a legal separation or a separation agreement will not cause the widow to lose the benefits provided for under the will. There is a situation, however, where jurisdictions differ. That is the case where the separation agreement expressly provides that each of the parties waive rights to the other's estate. While some states will recognize and enforce that stipulation, others will not, because in order to revoke a will, or the terms of a will, one must use the same formality as is required to make a valid will (signed in the presence of witnesses who attest to the signatures).

In other words, the stipulation in a separation agreement by both sides to give up inheritance rights may not be enough if an unrevoked will is still in existence at the testator's death.

There are situations that can affect inheritance even though no formal legal action has been commenced or no written agreement exists. In some jurisdictions, if the surviving spouse abandoned the deceased spouse, and that abandonment had continued until the time of death, the surviving spouse could lose the bequest provided for in the will.

Also, if the surviving spouse refused to support the deceased spouse during their lifetime, and had the means of support available, the bequest could be nullified.

Renunciation

Believe it or not, there are many who refuse to accept any part of a bequest made to them. This is done for several reasons, sometimes to avoid a creditor's claims against the estate and in others because of tax considerations. Also, it may very well happen that the recipient of a legacy in a will feels that members of the family were closer to the decedent and deserved a larger share.

Refusing the legacy is formally called a renunciation, and the rules vary in the different states as to how a renunciation becomes effective. The time periods vary, but essentially it must be signed in a formal document within a maximum period from the date of death. Also, the individual who renounces must not have accepted all or part of the property or any of its benefits.

In many jurisdictions, in the case of an infant, renunciation can be made only within the stated time period *after* the infant reaches the age of twenty-one. Moreover, as a general rule, a court will not approve of an infant executing a renunciation who has not reached legal adulthood.

May the disclaiming party change his or her mind? Yes, as long as it is done within the statutory period fixed by the law of your state.

The portion of the estate that has been renounced returns to the estate. The other recipients named in the will divide that share proportionately to their shares as set forth in the will.

One of the reasons set forth for executing a renunciation is to avoid tax liability. The Internal Revenue Service refers to renunciation as a disclaimer, but they mean the same thing. Uncle Sam allows the use of a disclaimer as a way to save your estate money. In the following pages, we will discuss this procedure.

Disclaimer Wills

Most of us don't do the necessary advance planning to avoid estate taxes. We try not to think about dying, and we are not comfortable with giving our money away during our lifetime just to avoid paying an estate tax.

There is a device called a disclaimer will that does not require that you rid yourself of a portion of your estate during your lifetime. When most middle-class couples write wills, each leaves everything to the surviving spouse. The problem is that if they set up their wills that way, their heirs can be hit with a heavy tax bill if the estate is more than $600,000.

Now, $600,000 may sound like a lot of money, but the truth of the matter is that if you are like most people, you have underestimated what the value of your estate will be at the time of your death. Real estate values, for example, are cyclical and could increase greatly from the time you write your will. Personal property can also increase in value. Also, it can be expected that you will have accumulated more assets. In other words, you may not have lived rich, but you may die rich—or at least richer than you thought you were—rich enough to encumber your estate with taxes that should have been avoided.

We are specifically talking about the estate tax. A married person can transfer an unlimited amount of property, including cash, to his or her spouse. But when one spouse dies, the surviving spouse can shield only $600,000 from estate taxes.

Of course, it is true that most couples have accumulated less than $600,000 *when they make their wills.* But we tend to make wills and never revise them. An estate worth $350,000 at the time of the making of the will could easily double in twenty years after making of the will, taking into consideration inflation and the two-income family. No thought is given to the possibility of exposing accumulated wealth to heavy taxes upon the death of a spouse. And heavy is the appropriate word. Examine the chart supplied by the Internal Revenue Service, and see for yourself how much of a cut Uncle Sam can take out of your estate if you and your spouse have accumulated more than $600,000.

TAXING ESTATES

Size of Estate	Marginal Tax Rate
$600,000 to $750,000	37%
$750,000 to $1 Million	39%
$1 Million to $1.25 Million	41%
$1.25 Million to $1.5 Million	43%
$1.5 Million to $2 Million	45%
$2 Million to $2.5 Million	49%
$2.5 Million to $3 Million	53%
$3 Million to $10 Million	55%
$10 Million to $21,040,000	55% (plus 5% surtax)

THE 1993 TAX LAW

For some time during the debate over the 1993 tax law, there was talk in Congress about reducing the estate tax rates. Unfortunately, talk is just what it was. Congress maintained the current rates as indicated in the chart. There have been no changes as far as estate taxes are concerned.

While very few of us can realistically expect to leave an estate of these proportions, it is conceivable that by the time we die our estate can be worth an amount in excess of $600,000. Let us continue with the example of the couple whose joint assets were much more than they had anticipated at the time of the death of one of the spouses. Assume that the estate is worth $700,000. The tax rate on the amount over $600,000 is 37%. Quite a bite, and quite a price to pay for not making advance arrangements through a disclaimer clause in the will or other tax avoidance procedures.

Here is how a disclaimer will works. Each spouse executes a disclaimer will. They leave everything to each other, but each specifies what will happen to property that is disclaimed. For example: "I give everything to my wife, Susan. If Susan should disclaim all or part of it, that portion goes into a trust from which she will receive the income, and on her death will go to our children."

Susan will have nine months from the date of his death to decide whether to disclaim any part of the bequest. In many instances, it takes an extended period of time to discover the true value of the estate. Once making that determination, she can disclaim any portion over $600,000, and that amount will be placed in trust. She will receive the income from that trust, and upon her death, the disclaimed portion will pass directly to her children. Assuming that the amount that *she* passes to her children is less than $600,000, both estates will pay zero estate tax.

This procedure has been sanctioned by the federal government. In 1976, when the federal estate and gift tax code was revised, a statute was added to clarify when the disclaimer was valid. It will be approved as long as the disclaimer is an unqualified refusal.

CHAPTER 14

Probate

Probate is the legal process in which your executor applies to the court for authority to carry out the terms and provisions of your will. Upon given that authority, he (or she) pays your outstanding debts and then distributes your property as your will dictates. He also has the authority to execute any needed documents in order to transfer title to all of the property.

In the probate proceeding, the court has the inherent power to intervene on behalf of minor children, and/or incompetents who are unable to handle their own affairs. In such instances, the court will appoint special guardians to protect their interests if the will does not so provide.

A will *must* go through the probate process in order for it to be enforceable. It must be validated as being authentic before the executor is given letters testamentary, which is the authority to proceed and carry out the deceased's intentions. Once the "letters" are issued, the executor then proceeds to carry out his or her duties in connection with the estate. He or she marshals (collects) the assets, pays the outstanding bills, and then distributes whatever remains to the distributees named in the will.

The process is begun when your executor files a petition, including your *original* will, with the probate court. Most states require that some formal notice of your death be published in a local newspaper for a specified period of time.

The purpose of this is to alert any possible creditors to present their claims of unpaid debts to the court. The notice also alerts anyone who thinks he or she should be a recipient of your estate.

Your executor at the same time, sends notification of your death to your named heirs—accompanied by a copy of your will.

Now that there has been public notice of your death, and heirs and possible creditors are notified, the court conducts its primary hearing—a month or two after publication and notice have been made by your executor. (Specified time varies from state to state.)

The first thing that the court must do is to validate your will. It must be ascertained that the will submitted was the correct will. (Many people execute more than one will. The basic law is that the last will revokes any and all wills previously made, unless otherwise stated.)

Next, the court must determine whether you were in a competent state of mind when you signed your will and whether it was witnessed according to the statutory requirements of your state. If your will is uncontested, all of this can generally be supplied by affidavits of the witnesses.

Once the will is validated, it is admitted into probate. The court will usually appoint the executor that you have named in your will to manage your estate. Besides inventorying your assets and determining their values, the executor must collect from your debtors what is owing to you and pay to your creditors what you owe. If your debtors do not pay what was lawfully owing to you during your lifetime, the executor has the power and the duty to commence and prosecute legal action to enforce collection. By the same token, if a claim is made by an alleged creditor that the executor feels has no merit, he or she will decline payment and defend the estate against legal action if instituted. In other words, whether bringing an action, or defending one, he or she stands in your shoes. Generally speaking, he or she is authorized to take any legal steps to protect or enhance the value of your estate. This includes application to Social Security, your union, or any fraternal organizations that you belonged to. You can make it easier for your executor by giving her or him a list of any group that may grant death benefits.

The letters testamentary previously referred to, which are issued to the executor once the will is validated, is the authority that the executor needs to act in your place, and in your name. The bank needs a copy to release the moneys in your bank account to her or him, as do brokerage houses, and government agencies from which he or she can claim benefits.

The extent of the executor's discretion in carrying out her or his duties depends on the state in which the probate proceedings are commenced and also on the type of action your executor is taking. For example, generally an executor has the right to invest a portion of your estate if you had given her or him that express authority to do so. However, state laws vary on whether the probate judge must approve those investments before they are made.

Executors are normally required to post a bond to secure the estate against negligence or even deliberate acts by the executor that might result in diminishing the estate's assets. Unfortunately, there have been instances where executors have been dishonest and raided the assets of the estate for their own purposes. The bonding company makes good on such losses. In some jurisdictions, you can direct in your will that no bond will be required for the faithful performance of your executor's duties. Certainly, if you have faith in the ability and the credibility of your executor, you should specifically make provision in your will to waive the requirement of a bond. Bonding companies may require notice of certain action taken by the executor and, in some instances, may insist on the right to be consulted before such actions are taken.

These precautions are to save the estate from incurring losses and also to save the bonding company from reimbursing the estate in the event these losses arise from the actions of the executor. They act as safeguards, and while they will not frustrate the intentions expressed in your will, they can delay the process. In addition, the executor's control and discretion may not be absolute. This may not be a problem for you, indeed it could give you additional peace of mind. On the other hand, you may have such total faith in your executor's ability and honesty that the expense of the bond or the delay it might cause would be totally unnecessary. It's your call.

The probate court will hold hearings (sometimes the hearings become full trials) on any conflicts related to the will. It is not uncommon for "heirs" to appear unheralded when it becomes known that your estate is larger than anyone thought it would be. These adversarial contests can be costly in time, because they can delay the probate process considerably, and in money, because the legal fees can be substantial.

Who are the people who contest a will? Some have legitimate claims, some specious, and it is up to the probate judge to decide whether the claims have merit. An example is the claim of a woman who lived with the male testator, provided services, and relied upon his representation that in return for her dedication and lifetime commitment of love and devotion and services, she would be rewarded in his will. Some of these claims have merit, some do not, but they are always problems because they require adjudication by the court.

Finally, after all the legal process is completed, the court will order a final hearing when your estate will be closed. It will order that all debts and approved claims as well as costs and fees be paid. Distribution will then be made to the distributees named in the will.

That in essence is the general procedure of probate. There is an exception to the process in many states that applies to small estates. These can be administered quickly and *do not require the services of a lawyer.* The limits on the entire estate that qualify for this process are low —ranging from $15,000 to $25,000 depending on the state where the decedents assets were located, but nevertheless, there are many such estates.

If you are an executor of such a will, check with the local probate court to determine whether the estate qualifies. If it does, the clerk will provide you with the forms and help you if necessary. The filing fee will be minimum, and the process should be completed quickly.

If your estate is fairly substantial, there are certain costs that cannot be avoided. Filing fees, publication costs, bond premiums, and executor and attorney fees will be paid before your heirs receive any part of your estate. The fees of attorneys are especially difficult to predict. Some states require the probate judge to approve payment of any fees by the estate. Others have a maximum fee schedule. But there is no rule that an agreement cannot be made between the attorney and your executor to charge less than the maximum. It would be wise for your executor to discuss this with the attorney before he or she is retained. You can also make a provision in your will that a specific attorney be retained to represent the executor, if you have confidence that the attorney will treat you fairly.

Heirs

In describing the probate process, we often use the term heir, which can be confusing. Technically, only persons designated by statute are heirs. For example, examine the sample Intestacy Chart which, if you haven't written a will, specifically defines who your heirs are and the percentage of your estate that they will receive under certain circumstances.

The recipients that you have named in your will could be called beneficiaries, or legatees, or devisees, but need not necessarily be heirs. Children, for example, are natural heirs of the deceased. Yet the law in many states does not require that they be provided for in the will.

If you recall, this is not the case with the widow (or the husband, if he is the surviving spouse). She has the right of election, meaning, that unless she receives in the will an amount equal to what the statute decrees is the minimum, she can elect against the will and take the amount that the law guarantees her.

There are some states, however, that also give children the right of election to claim a portion of the estate if they are not mentioned in the will. In California, children unprovided for in the will, or who have not had an advancement of their inheritance during the testator's lifetime, may also be given the same right of election to take their state-mandated intestate share. This is what the law calls a "qualified" right. It is not available to the children if the testator makes it clear in his or her will that he or she is omitting them intentionally. For example, if his or her will contains something like: "In making this will I have taken into consideration my two children, John and Jane, who have given me nothing but aggravation and helped to put me in my grave, and I therefore leave them nothing." Nothing is what they will get. Actually, the testator does not have to reveal his or her motives. Any clear expression of intention to exclude children is sufficient to defeat their right of election.

Assume a much healthier situation, where the concern is for minor children who, through catastrophe or fate, lose their parents while they are still minors. When the estate goes into probate after the parents' death, the court will usually go along with the guardian that was named in the will to raise and provide for the children, but it doesn't have to. There is a legal maxim enforced by the probate courts that holds that minor children are wards of the court, meaning, among other things, that the court's discretion in securing their welfare supercedes all others. If the court, for valid reason, believes that the best interests of the minor will not be served by continuing with the guardian that has been named in the will, the court will name another.

There are situations where the court must appoint guardians even if both parents are alive and healthy. Grandparents, uncles, aunts, and others with good intentions, may leave money, stock, real estate, CD's, and other items of value to a minor child. If the child is still a minor when that individual dies, the court must appoint a guardian because the minor's interests must be protected. While the guardian would probably be the parent, an attorney will have to represent the minor at any court hearing. Until the minor reaches legal age, none of the properties left in his or her name can be sold, nor money spent, without the approval of the court.

Based on the guardian requirement, it may not be a great idea to make your minor child the direct beneficiary of a life insurance policy. If, after you die, the life insurance company is aware that the named beneficiary is still a minor, it will probably not pay out the benefits, unless proof of a court-appointed guardian is submitted. The same difficulty could result when a minor is a named beneficiary in a pension plan or IRA. The better procedure is to name a trustee to receive the proceeds in trust for the minor child only in the event that you die before the child reaches majority. Upon reaching adulthood, you of course will substitute his or her name on the policy as the designated beneficiary.

One more thing. If you can help it, never (repeat, never) make a minor a joint owner with you on real estate, personal property such as automobiles, or stocks or bonds. For the only way to sell them would be through the approval of the court through guardianship. No matter what the property is—no matter what the sale price—the transaction has to have the court's OK. This will entail a delay and unnecessary legal fees by setting up a probate guardianship, even though you are alive.

Finally, a court guardianship stays in effect until the minor child becomes an adult. The age varies from eighteen to twenty-one, depending on the law of your state, but on that birthday the guardianship goes out of existence and the former minor assumes full and complete ownership of the property.

Probate Costs

The cost of probate depends upon the size of your estate and the probate fees that are fixed by law in your state. Fiduciaries (executors, guardians, trustees) are also compensated according to your state's law. The following is an example of the New York State Schedule:

5% on the first $100,000
4% on the next $200,000
3% on the next $700,000
2.5% from $1 million to $5 million
2% over $5 million

With these fees included, the probate costs could range from five to ten percent of your gross estate. That is why many recommend the use of the living trust, instead of the will and probate process, as a viable alternative. By using this trust, depending on the size of your estate, you may avoid some of the expenses and other problems that come with probate. Yet, there are advantages and disadvantages to both. Before we discuss the pros and cons, let us understand just what the living trust is and how it may serve your purpose.

CHAPTER 15

Living Trusts

Instead of having your property pass on after your death, you can execute a written document that allows you to transfer ownership of your property during your lifetime *and* after you die. The instrument is called a living trust.

Actually, you perform what lawyers refer to as a "legal fiction," all perfectly legitimate and proper. You transfer the property from your name to a "trust." You don't lose control over it. It remains yours, but it is in the trust's name. Technically, the trust is the owner. By providing for disposition of the assets of the trust on your death, you can keep your estate out of probate.

If you create the trust—if the assets referred to are yours—then you are called the settlor (or the grantor or trustor.) If you and your spouse set up one trust together, you are joint settlors.

The trustee is the individual or institution that manages and administers the trust, with the power and authority to invest, collect accounts receivable, pay bills,

223

and do any and all other acts that you would normally perform in preserving and enhancing your assets. You can name yourself as trustee, and if married can name your spouse as co-trustee, giving each the right to act for the other. If either of you should become incompetent or die, the other automatically controls the trust property, without the requirement of court approval or intervention. Trust income may be received by either or both of you during the life of the trust, or you may provide that trust income go to a third party.

If you are the sole trustee, or if you and your spouse are co-trustees, a third individual should be involved. He or she is called a successor trustee and will carry out your instructions as they appear in the trust document. This is required should you become incompetent as the sole trustee, or in the case of a married couple, if both trustees die in a common disaster or become incompetent to perform the services that the trust requires. There should never be a time when a trustee is not in actual existence.

If the assets of your estate can be simply managed, there is no need for you to retain any individual or institution to be trustee. At the same time, you or the one you name must be capable of carrying out important responsibilities and making vital decisions. These are all your life's assets. You may love your trustee dearly, but if he or she does not have the expertise to manage your affairs, then it would be wise to hire a bank or other financial institution that does. Their services don't come cheaply, but remember, you are paying for their professional guidance, and depending on the amount of your estate and its complexity, you should be sure that whomever you choose can handle the job.

The person or persons who receive your property upon your death are called beneficiaries. They can be relatives, friends, or even charitable foundations. There is no limit on whom you can name. Trusts, like wills, can be modified but seldom are, so it would be prudent to name an alternate beneficiary or beneficiaries if the one you name dies before you do.

If you have minor children, there are certain special provisions that you must make to prevent the court from taking control should you and your spouse die while they are still minors. Upon the death of the settlor, the trust ends automatically. To prevent the possibility of the children's inheritance winding up under the supervision of the probate court, you must include a provision in your trust that upon your death (or the death of your spouse who is your co-trustee) the property designated to become the property of your minor children is immediately transferred into another trust for your children. This, of course, will only take effect if they are still minors when you die. Once reaching adulthood they can receive their inheritance outright.

There is just no way that you can create a living trust without the services of an attorney, and one that has more than a passing knowledge of trusts and estate planning. Besides drawing the document so that it conforms with the requirements of your state's law, he or she can advise you as to the best way to transcribe your intentions in the trust. If it is not drawn correctly, there could be complications that you had originally set out to avoid.

Once you sign the trust and the document is notarized, you then have the task of transferring *all* of your property into the trust. *All* is the key word here, because anything that you do not transfer will have to go through probate, and to that extent you will have defeated your purpose. If the property is real estate, you change the form of deed to a quit claim deed, (sometimes referred to as a trust transfer or correction deed). The deed will change the title from your name, "Sam Jones," to "Sam Jones as Trustee under Trust, dated (the date the trust is signed)." The deed is then filed, and the transfer of property is then in effect. However, in going through this procedure there is something that you have to guard against.

If you recall, reference was made to the pros and cons of making a trust. We will discuss them in detail later, but one of the problems that can arise from this type of real estate transfer is with the title company. Here is the experience of a friend.

As all homeowners know, when you purchase your home, you also purchase a title policy that insures you against claims and lawsuits from any person or persons who allege a claim against your property, such as a prior mortgage lien or a boundary dispute. After transferring his property into the living trust, (he named his son as trustee), my friend filed the new deed and then requested that the title company change the name of the insured to correspond to the new designation. In other words, he requested that the *trust* be the named insured instead of him.

The title company refused to make the change, for reasons known only to them. We can only guess that they believed that the transfer of title into a trust could expose them to new claims or lawsuits not contemplated when the original policy was issued. Whether their fears were justified or groundless, they could not be compelled to change the named insured from an individual to a trust.

Obviously, he should not have assumed that the title company would go along with the transfer of title and neither should you. Before entering into a trust agreement, inquire of any insurance carrier that covers you in your individual names whether there will be any problem with the transfer. In most cases there won't be, but it is safer to know in advance.

Trust Flexibility

Trust moneys accumulate, and naturally it would be better to keep the trust assets in tact to acquire an adequate estate to pass on to your beneficiaries when you die. But it is important to know that you can withdraw sums as circumstances require. You are not locked in. If, for example, your child is the named beneficiary of the trust and an emergency situation arises where you want to advance moneys to that child, you are free to do so. You can do this in the form of a loan against the inheritance. You can also provide for your trustee to have the same discretion after you die. You of course can limit the discretion of the trustee to make these decisions, or you can give her or him authority to use her or his judgment in advancing sums for any purpose.

This discretion becomes especially important if you have some reason to believe that your child does not possess the responsibility to receive his or her inheritance. Unfortunately, this may be the case if there is a drug problem or some other addiction that you could reasonably foresee leading to dissipation of the assets. This problem can be avoided by providing that the inheritance remain in trust until the child reaches an age of greater maturity. You can specify that until your child reaches a certain age, the assets will remain in trust, and the trustee will provide for your child's needs and have the power to manage the estate, including the right to invest. You may also provide that the assets remain in trust for the lifetime of your child (the income of which he or she will receive) and, upon the child's death, be given outright to a third party such as a grandchild. You can also limit the powers of the trustee, but whatever your intent, the limits must be spelled out clearly so that the trustees and the beneficiaries know the full extent of the trustee's authority.

Your options are almost unlimited. Naturally, when you make any choice of disposition, one of the considerations is the tax consequences. Therefore, before making any such provision, consult your attorney or accountant as to what tax consequences, if any, would result.

Estate Tax Avoidance

We discussed disclaimer wills as a method of avoiding the heavy estate tax (see Taxing Estates Chart, page 210). There is another way to accomplish that desirable result through a trust, or rather two trusts.

If you recall, the marital deduction allows you to leave all of your estate—no matter what the amount—to your surviving spouse, *tax free.* As long as it goes to the surviving spouse, the estate tax does not apply. But when your surviving spouse dies, all of it (what you left her or him and what she or he accumulated after your death) less the $600,000 exemption, can be taxed before your heirs receive it.

Here is how you can double that exemption, and make $1,200,000 free of estate taxes for the benefit of your beneficiaries. Remember that *each* spouse is entitled to the $600,000 exemption. Therefore, you and your spouse set up a separate trust for each. Arrange it so that each of you owns one half of the assets, with the aim of putting a cap on $600,000 of assets for each. When one of the spouses dies, the trust of the deceased spouse is entitled to the $600,000 exemption. When the surviving spouse dies, his or her trust is also entitled to the $600,000 exemption. The combined assets of both trusts are then distributed to the beneficiaries, and assuming the total amount does not exceed $1.2 million, there should be no estate tax.

A Cautionary Note: The trust must be specific in its language to comply with the Internal Revenue Code to achieve this result. That is why when you choose your attorney to draw these trust agreements, be sure that he or she has an expertise in the construction of trusts and an awareness of the tax code provisions that apply to estate taxes.

Pros and Cons

You will see many books and other publications on the market that extol the living trust as the end all—saving you the expenses and other inconveniences of probate and simplifying the process. The problem is that the benefits of the living trust do not apply to everyone and every possible situation that your estate could encounter. Let us go over the pros and cons of the living trust.

Pros

The outstanding advantage is that it avoids the costs and the delays of probate, which also means that your affairs remain private. A will must be filed and therefore becomes a public record. A living trust need not be filed, and therefore is not subject to public inspection.

Distribution to your beneficiaries is accomplished in a much shorter time. If you recall, the probate process can be lengthy. This might be an important consideration if hardship could result from an extended delay.

While technically the trust can be contested on the basis of fraud or duress or other legal grounds, it is more difficult to contest than a will, where publication must be made that could be an invitation to all who can conceive of claims against the estate.

The relatively short period it takes to carry out the provisions of your trust can save your family the emotional stress that this entails.

Minor children will not have to be placed under court supervision. Guardians for the children can be provided for in the trust and will need neither court input nor approval. (Nevertheless, if an issue is raised as to the competency of a guardian by an interested party, the court has the inherent power to inquire into those allegations.)

The trust can be completely flexible, and you can modify, alter, or even revoke the trust at anytime in your life. The advantage over a will is self-evident—you can't change your mind or realize a mistake after you are dead.

You can reduce estate taxes or even eliminate them by using the "two trust" procedure. However, the disclaimer will, which we discussed previously, is another method of tax avoidance that is a perfectly legitimate procedure.

The living trust gives you a valid and effective way to protect your prenuptial property. Anything placed in it before you marry is separate and apart from property that had been accumulated during your marriage. As long as you keep it separate, it will be protected against spousal claims in divorce court. Unfortunately, statistics show that more and more marriages can break up, and the protection of prenuptial assets becomes an important consideration. Confining premarital property to the living trust is an efficient method of protection for you or your spouse, if that is your intention.

These are some of the many advantages of the living trust. The trust does have its disadvantages, which may or may not apply to you, but you should at least be made aware of them.

Cons

We've already discussed a situation in which the title company refused to change the name of the insured from the individual name into the trust name. While that is not a common problem, you may find the changing of title of ownership from your name into the trust name a long and tedious effort. Keep in mind that unless you place all of your assets in the trust, those that you have not must go into probate after your death. To that extent you would have defeated your purpose. Be prepared, then, to go through the various procedures that different institutions require to change titles.

If you place your real property in a trust, you may not find it easy to refinance your mortgage. There is a reluctance on the part of some lenders to go along with the change of title, because they fear the possibility that there may be a restriction on your trustee in mortgaging or selling property. A provision in your trust agreement that gives your trustee those explicit powers without requiring your prior consent should satisfy the lenders, but even then they may be reluctant to mortgage anything in the trust name, especially if your prior mortgage was in your name or in the names of you and your spouse.

When your estate goes through the probate process, there is a limit on the time that your creditors can assert a claim after probate is commenced. If due notice of probate has been complied with pursuant to the laws of your state, and if those creditors don't submit their claims within that time period, they are out of luck. But this is not so in a living trust. The regular statute of limitations would apply, which could be as much as six years in some states, and your creditors could sue your beneficiaries even after the assets have been distributed to them.

The following could be *the* reason why you would not want to use the living trust. In some states, your home is automatically protected from creditors when you file for bankruptcy. If your property has been placed in a living trust, for your benefit, *you will lose that protection.* None of us anticipates the sorry prospect of filing for bankruptcy at anytime in our lives, and if you feel secure and are confident that it won't happen, then don't consider this a problem. But on the other hand, you know your own circumstances, and if bankruptcy is even a remote possibility, then consult with your attorney as to how your state's laws would affect the retention of your home—your most valuable possession.

There are other pros and cons, of course; I have listed those I think would be of most interest and perhaps affect your decision. Scientists claim that each snowflake is different in design and form, and the same is true for all of us—we are individuals who have problems unique to ourselves. What works for one may not work for the other. Will/probate or trust? Weigh the pros and cons, consult with your attorney if you have some questions, and make the final determination yourself.

CHAPTER 16

Wills and Trusts:
Questions and Answers

Q *Must my will be notarized?*

A Your signature at the end of the will need not be notarized. However, although not required, it is recommended that the attesting witnesses sign an affidavit (see page 247), which must be notarized. This affidavit might save your heirs a lot of trouble if for some reason the witnesses are not available when your executor submits the will for probate.

Q *Why can't I avoid going through probate or entering into a trust by simply putting my property in joint names with my spouse or my children?*

A You can do that as long as you are aware of possible consequences that would not carry out your intent. This is usually done by placing the property in joint names with full ownership to the survivor. Upon the death of one, title to the property automatically vests in the survivor without the necessity of going

235

through probate. That's fine, but something more must be done.

To be certain that your property, and the additional property accumulated by your joint owner, is not submitted to probate, the survivor must make a further joint ownership agreement with someone else. If that is not done, your combined estates must go into probate upon the death of the survivor. The end result will be a delay of the probate process, but not an avoidance of it.

Q *One of my children has displeased me during my lifetime. May I disinherit that child and still provide for my other children?*

A In most states, the only member of the family that you cannot disinherit is your surviving spouse. However, in some states your child can demand an intestate share unless you specifically state in your will that you are omitting that child from any inheritance.

Q *Assume that I die in State A but part of my estate is located in State B. Is the will then probated under the laws of State A?*

A Not as to the real property. The rule is that your estate is probated under the laws of the state where the real property is located. If the personal property that you describe in your will (cash, stock, jewelry, art, antiques, etc.) is in the state where you died, it will be probated under the laws of that state. But the process must be gone through again if the real property is located elsewhere.

Q *Must the will be in any special form or drawn on any special legal paper?*

A As long as you were in a competent state of mind when you drew the will and you complied with the laws of the state where your estate is submitted for probate (witnessed by required number, dated, signature at the end, etc.), and as long as the writing is legible and your written intent is coherent, you can write your will on a brown paper bag and it will be accepted for probate.

Q *Can I avoid probate by executing a durable power of attorney?*

A No. Any power of attorney is automatically revoked on your death. The "durable" part only means that your agent will have the power to carry out your wishes in the event you become physically or mentally incompetent to make decisions for yourself.

Q *Assume that I die in an automobile accident that is caused by a negligent driver and my estate collects the life insurance. Can my estate still bring an action for negligence?*

A Absolutely. The receipt by your heirs of the life insurance proceeds or any other death benefits does not preclude your estate from commencing a lawsuit for wrongful death. Your executor is the plaintiff representing your estate.

Q *Can I set up a trust like a living trust in my will?*

A Yes, the procedure is the same. If, as in a living

trust, it is your intent to keep the corpus (principal) of the trust in tact for a period of time and have the beneficiaries receive the income from the trust, you can make that provision. You also have the option of having the trust end after a specified time or after a stated event, such as the beneficiary reaching a certain age. You can also provide that upon the death of the first beneficiary, the trust will pass on to a second beneficiary. The formation of the trust is similar to the living trust. You must name a trustee (he or she can also be your executor) to carry out your intent.

Q *What happens if the probate court finds that my will was not validly drawn?*

A If the court makes that determination, your estate will be probated under the laws of intestacy (as if no will was ever drawn). Property will be distributed according to the intestacy schedule in your state. (See page 199 for New York State example.)

Q *What happens if I make a will but don't name an executor?*

A The Court will then name an executor, usually based on some family relationship. However, the court need not appoint an executor from a specified schedule, such as provided for in the intestacy chart. By the same token, if no guardian is named in your will for infant beneficiaries in the event that you die while they are still minors, the court will appoint such a guardian. In those instances, the probate judge has the discretion to choose the individual who would best serve the interests of the estate and the interests of the minors, and they could be the same person.

Q *What kind of bite do probate fees take out of my estate?*
A It depends upon the laws of the state in which your will is probated. Each state regulates the court fees (filing fees, etc.) and the percentages that the executors and attorneys can receive. New York seems to take the highest cut of the pie. An estate of $100,000 could be hit with a total probate cost of approximately $10,000, while in California the same estate would cost approximately $6500. Naturally, as the estate grows larger, the disparity is larger. An estate of $1 million in New York could result in a total probate bill of $60,000, while in California, the same estate costs approximately $40,000 to probate. But keep in mind that these are only general figures. If there are complications that require your executor and/or her or his attorney to provide more services than are ordinarily contemplated, their requests for additional compensation will be approved more times than not. Also, additional costs can emerge during probate. For example, if real property (real estate) is involved and must be sold in order to carry out your intent, there are additional appraisal and publication expenses.

Q *Can I make a bequest in my will that is conditional on some future event or happening?*

A Yes, you may make a conditional bequest, as long as the condition is reasonable and clearly spelled out. For example: "My son John will receive the sum of $25,000 the day that he graduates from college" is a reasonable condition and will be enforced by the court as long as there is no disability that could reasonably prevent John from graduating college.

On the other hand, let us suppose the bequest reads: "My son John will receive the sum of $25,000 the day that he is awarded the Nobel Prize." That is an inherently unreasonable condition and all other things being equal, the court will ignore it and approve John's bequest.

Q *How can I protect my estate against unfounded claims by "heirs" that I never intended to reward in my will?*

A Unfortunately, there is nothing you can do to prevent such claims. Once you have died, supposed heirs may come from anywhere. The usual claim is that your love and affection for them was so great that failure to provide had to be the result of fraud or duress practiced by other members of the family, the lawyer, the butler, or someone else intent on depriving them of their inheritance. While some of these claims could have merit, most of them don't. Moreover, they are extremely difficult to prove to the judge's satisfaction, and most are eventually dismissed. However, they can be a cause of extra expense and delay in bringing the estate to a close.

Q *I see many "Do-It-Yourself Will Kits" advertised. Can I safely use the forms in those books and save an attorney's fee?*

A They serve a purpose, up to a point. While providing you with a general format, you must remember that they are generic, across-the-board samples and may not comply with specific legal requirements in your state. There is nothing wrong with saving the legal fee for drawing a simple will, which does not involve complicated situations, but even then, I would advise you to consult an attorney just to be sure that you haven't included or omitted anything that could defeat the purpose of your will. The consultation fee will be much less than the fee he or she would have charged for drawing the will, and your peace of mind should be worth that small investment.

Q *If the original will is lost, does that mean it cannot be probated?*

A Not necessarily. Some states have statutory provisions in the case of lost wills, but most require "clear proof" of the terms of the will. Clear proof means different things to different people. A lot depends upon the quality of the testimony at the hearing and how the witnesses who testify impress the court. "Clear proof" could involve the attorney who drew the will submitting a copy of it and testifying to its validity, combined with the attesting witnesses' testimony that they saw you sign it and heard the attorney ask you whether it was your last will and testament.

CHAPTER 17

Sample Will

If you recall, the recommendation made at the outset was that everyone should have a will. If you feel that a living trust would be better suited to you, then so be it. But one thing is clear—you will be courting trouble and confusion for your heirs if you die without first executing a written instrument that sets forth your clear intent as to how your estate is to be distributed after you die. Having your estate disposed of by your state's intestacy laws can be a grim prospect.

Remember, your spouse is the only relative who *must* receive an inheritance under the law, but if there is no will or trust, other individuals related to you will be beneficiaries under the intestacy laws regardless of your feelings toward them. The hard fact is that we sometimes become estranged from some members of our family during our lifetime. It's not pleasant, but it happens. On the other hand, we often develop relationships with others who are not blood relatives but with whom we share love and respect. It is natural for us to seek to reward those who have demonstrated kindness and devotion—relatives or not. Under intestacy, they receive nothing, and those who we would not want to be beneficiaries could inherit it all.

Equally distressing is the possibility that your minor children or grandchildren will receive their bequests only under court supervision. A guardian would have to be appointed to protect their interests. That individual could be a stranger or a member of the family whom you would not trust or prefer to assume that responsibility. This can cause an unwanted and unnecessary expense to the estate. More important, however, is the uncomforting realization that you could lose control. This can be eliminated by naming a guardian of your choice in a will or a trust.

The following is a sample will. It is basic. It does not cover the hundreds of unique situations that could apply to your estate. It is submitted to give you a general idea of how a will appears and the general form it takes. It creates a trust for minor children and the naming of a trustee. It describes the powers of the trustee and the executor, which you should be familiar with. You will notice that the attestation clause at the end, followed by the witnesses' signatures, is verbose and somewhat repetitive. However, the precise language can be very important if there are any future contests based upon your competency or understanding of what you were doing.

SAMPLE WILL

Last Will and Testament of
John Smith

I, JOHN SMITH, residing at 000 E. Clark Street, New York, New York, being of sound and disposing mind and memory do hereby make, publish, and declare this as my last Will and Testament, hereby revoking all former Wills and Codicils at any time heretofore made by me.

First: I hereby direct the payment of all my just debts and funeral expenses incurred by me in the administration of my Estate as soon as possible after my demise.

Second: I hereby give, devise, and bequeath the sum of $50,000 to my beloved son, WILLIAM SMITH.

Third: I hereby give, devise, and bequeath the sum of $50,000 to my beloved daughter, JANE SMITH.

Fourth: I hereby give, devise, and bequeath the remainder of my property, whether real, personal, or mixed, wheresover situated and whatsoever consisting to my beloved wife, MARY SMITH, to be hers absolutely and forever.

Fifth: In the event that my beloved wife, MARY SMITH, should predecease me, or if we should die in a common occurrence where it cannot be determined which survived the other, then in such event I hereby give, devise, and bequeath the remainder of my property, whether real, personal or mixed to my beloved children, WILLIAM SMITH and JANE SMITH, share and share alike, to be theirs, absolutely and forever.

Sixth: In the event that both of my beloved children, WILLIAM SMITH and JANE SMITH, or either of them, shall not have reached the age of twenty-one years at the time of my death, I hereby give, devise, and bequeath any property which they, or either of them is designated to receive, to my brother ALEXANDER SMITH, in trust nevertheless, for the following uses and purposes:

(continued)

(a) To invest and reinvest all of my said property and to apply so much of the net income therefrom and so much of the principal thereof as may be necessary for the support, maintenance, and education of my said children or either of them until he or she reaches the age of twenty-one years, and at that time to transfer and pay over to him or her, his or her share of the principal and income so accumulated and the trust for the said beneficiary will terminate.

Seventh: I hereby nominate, constitute and appoint my brother, ALEXANDER SMITH, to be Executor under this Will, and I direct that he shall not be required to furnish any bond or security for the faithful performance of his duties as executor.

Eighth: I hereby authorize and empower my said executor to mortgage for any purpose, sell, exchange, or otherwise dispose of any property and real estate which I may die seized or possessed or which I may be entitled, or in which I or any trust created herein have any interest, at either private or public sale, for such price and upon such terms, including sales on credit, with or without security and conditions as my said executor shall deem most advantageous to my estate or any trust and to execute, acknowledge and deliver all such deeds, agreements, and other instruments in writing necessary or expedient to effect the foregoing. Pending a sale or other disposition of any real property, my executor may lease such property for such term or terms as he deems advisable. These shall be continuing powers and may be exercised at any time and from time to time during the administration of my estate, or the duration of the trust created hereunder.

IN WITNESS WHEREOF, I have hereunto set my hand and seal and identified each of these (3) sheets of this, my last Will and Testament, by placing my signature at the end of this, my last Will and Testament, on the_____day of_____, 1994

JOHN SMITH

(continued)

The foregoing instrument consisting of this and two additional sheets, was subscribed by the Testator, in his name, JOHN SMITH, at the end thereof and in the presence of each of us on the_____day of_____, 1994, and at the time of making such subscription, by him, the Testator declared the foregoing instrument so subscribed by him to be his last Will and Testament and he requested us and each of us to sign our names as witnesses thereof, which we hereupon do at the end of the will at the request of the said Testator and in his presence and of each other this_____day of_____, 1994, after this attestation clause was read aloud in the presence of and the hearing of the said Testator and consented to by him.

_____   Residing at _____

_____   Residing at _____

_____   Residing at _____

Subscribed and sworn to before me this ____ day of _____, 199__.

(Seal Affixed)   Notary Public